THE MIRACLE OF RIGHT THOUGHT
BY ORISON SWETT MARDEN

A SELECT LIST OF SUN BOOKS TITLES

ORISON SWETT MARDEN BOOKS

AN IRON WILL
CHARACTER: The Grandest Thing in the World
THE EXCEPTIONAL EMPLOYEE
EVERY MAN A KING or MIGHT IN MIND-
  MASTERY
HE CAN WHO THINKS HE CAN
THE HOUR OF OPPORTUNITY
HOW THEY SUCCEEDED
HOW TO GET WHAT YOU WANT

THE MIRACLE OF RIGHT THOUGHT
THE OPTIMISTIC LIFE
PEACE, POWER, AND PLENTY
PUSHING TO THE FRONT 2 VOL SET
THE SECRET OF ACHIEVEMENT
SELLING THINGS
THE VICTORIOUS ATTITUDE
WHY GROW OLD?
YOU CAN, BUT WILL YOU?

JAMES ALLEN BOOKS

ABOVE LIFE'S TURMOIL
ALL THESE THINGS ADDED
AS A MAN THINKETH
EIGHT PILLARS OF PROSPERITY
FROM POVERTY TO POWER
THE LIFE TRIUMPHANT
LIGHT ON LIFE'S DIFFICULTIES
MAN: KING OF MIND, BODY AND
  CIRCUMSTANCE

THE MASTERY OF DESTINY
MEDITATIONS: A YEAR BOOK
MORNING AND EVENING THOUGHTS
OUT FROM THE HEART
THROUGH THE GATE OF GOOD
THE WAY OF PEACE
PERSONALITY: ITS CULTIVATION AND
  POWER AND HOW TO ATTAIN
  (by Lily L. Allen)

RALPH WALDO TRINE BOOKS

CHARACTER BUILDING THOUGHT POWER
EVERY LIVING CREATURE or Heart Training
  Through the Animal World
IN THE FIRE OF THE HEART
THE GREATEST THING EVER KNOWN

THE HIGHER POWERS OF MIND & SPIRIT
THE MAN WHO KNEW
ON THE OPEN ROAD - Being Some Thoughts
  and a Little Creed of Wholesome Living
THIS MYSTICAL LIFE OF OURS

ADDITIONAL IMPORTANT TITLES

BEING AND BECOMING: Principles and Practices of the Science of Spirit by F.L. Holmes.
CREATIVE MIND by Ernest S. Holmes.
HEALTH AND WEALTH FROM WITHIN by William E. Towne.
A MESSAGE TO GARCIA and Other Essays by Elbert Hubbard.
POSITIVE THOUGHTS ATTRACT SUCCESS by Mary A. Dodson and Ella E. Dodson.
THE SCIENCE OF GETTING RICH: or Financial Success Through Creative Thought.
SELF MASTERY THROUGH CONSCIOUS AUTOSUGGESTION by Emile Coué.
HOW TO PRACTICE SUGGESTION AND AUTOSUGGESTION by Emile Coué.
MY METHOD by Emile Coué.
THE SUCCESS PROCESS by Brown Landone.
THE GIFT OF THE SPIRIT by Prentice Mulford.
THE GIFT OF UNDERSTANDING by Prentice Mulford.
THOUGHT FORCES by Prentice Mulford.   THOUGHTS ARE THINGS by Prentice Mulford.
VISUALIZATION AND CONCENTRATION and How to Choose a Career by F.L. Holmes.

**For a list of all currently available Sun Books Inspirational Titles,
write to: Inspiration Catalog, PO Box 5588, Santa Fe NM 87502-5588**

M JUL 97   NEW-PAGE.PM5

THE MARDEN
INSPIRATIONAL BOOKS

Be Good to Yourself

Choosing a Career

Conquest of Worry

Every Man a King

The Exceptional Employee

Getting On

He Can Who Thinks He Can

How They Succeeded

How to Get What You Want

How to Succeed

Joys of Living

Keeping Fit

Little Visits With Great
  Americans

Love's Way

Making Friends With Our
  Nerves

Making Life a Masterpiece

Making Yourself

Masterful Personality

Miracle of Right Thought

Optimistic Life

Peace, Power, and Plenty

Progressive Business Man

Pushing to the Front

Rising in the World

Round Pegs in Square Holes

Secret of Achievement

Self-Investment

Selling Things

Success- A Book of Ideals

Success Fundamentals

Training for Efficiency

Victorious Attitude

Winning Out

Woman and the Home

You Can, But Will You?

The Young Man Entering
  Business

SPECIAL BOOKS AND BOOKLETS

An Iron Will   Opportunity   Self-Discovery

Economy   Cheerfulness   Hints for Young Writers

Thrift   Success Nuggets

I Had a Friend   Why Grow Old?

Not the Salary, But the Opportunity

Ambition and Success   The Power of Personality

Good Manners- A Passport to Success   Thoughts About Character

Thoughts About Cheerfulness

The Life Story of Orison Swett Marden
By Margaret Connolly

Orison S. Marden

The Miracle of Right Thought

BY

ORISON SWETT MARDEN

Author of
"Peace, Power, and Plenty," "He Can Who Thinks He
Can," "Getting On," etc.

Editor of *Success Magazine*

"All human duty is boiled down to this:
'Learn what to think and think it.'"

SUN BOOKS
Sun Publishing Company

First Sun Books Printing...1996

Copyright © 1996 By Sun Publishing Company

COPYRIGHT, 1910,
BY ORISON SWETT MARDEN.

———

Published December, 1910.

Eighteenth Thousand

Sun Books
are Published by
Sun Publishing Company
P.O. Box 5588 Santa Fe,
NM 87502-5588 U.S.A.

ISBN: 0-89540-311-0

TO MY FRIEND

EDWIN MARKHAM

PREFACE

HE demand during its first two years for nearly an edition a month of " Peace, Power, and Plenty," the author's last book, and its republication in England, Germany, and France, together with the hundreds of letters received from readers, many of whom say that it has opened up a new world of possibilities to them by enabling them to discover and make use of forces within themselves which they never before knew they possessed, all seem to be indications of a great hunger of humanity for knowledge of what we may call the new gospel of optimism and love, the philosophy of sweetness and light, which aims to show how one can put himself beyond the possibility of self-wreckage from ignorance, deficiencies, weaknesses, and even vicious tendencies, and which promises long-looked-for relief from the slavery of poverty, limitation, ill-health, and all kinds of success and happiness enemies.

The author's excuse for putting out this companion volume, " The Miracle of Right Thought," is the hope of arousing the reader to discover the wonderful forces in the Great Within of himself which, if he could unlock and utilize, would lift him out of the region of anxiety and worry, eliminate most, if not all, of the discords and frictions of life, and enable him to make of himself everything he ever imagined he could and longed to become.

The book teaches the divinity of right desire; it

tries to show that the Creator never mocked us with yearnings for that which we have no ability or possibility of attaining; that our heart longings and aspirations are prophecies, forerunners, indications of the existence of the obtainable reality, that there is an actual powerful creative force in our legitimate desires, in believing with all our hearts that, no matter what the seeming obstacles, we shall be what we were intended to be and do what we were made to do; in visualizing, affirming things as we would *like* to have them, as they *ought* to be; in holding the ideal of that which we wish to come true, and only that, the ideal of the man or woman we would like to become, in thinking of ourselves as absolutely perfect beings possessing superb health, a magnificent body, a vigorous constitution, and a sublime mind. It teaches that we should strangle every idea of deficiency, imperfection, or inferiority, and however much our apparent conditions of discord, weaknesses, poverty, and ill-health may seem to contradict, cling tenaciously to our vision of perfection, to the divine image of ourselves, the ideal which the Creator intended for His children; should affirm vigorously that there can be no inferiority or depravity about the man God made, for in the truth of our being we are perfect and immortal; because our mental attitude, what we habitually think, furnishes a pattern which the life processes are constantly weaving, outpicturing in the life.

The book teaches that fear is the great human curse, that it blights more lives, makes more people unhappy and unsuccessful than any other one thing; that worry-thoughts, fear-thoughts, are so many malignant forces within us poisoning the very sources of life, destroying harmony, ruining efficiency, while the opposite thoughts heal, soothe instead of irritate, and increase efficiency and multiply mental power; that every cell in the body suffers or is a gainer, gets a life impulse or a death impulse, from every thought that enters the mind, for we tend to grow into the image of that which we think about most, love the best; that the body is really our thoughts, moods, convictions objectified, outpictured, made visible to the eye. "The Gods we worship write their names on our faces." The face is carved from within by invisible tools; our thoughts, our moods, our emotions are the chisels. It is the table of contents of our life history; a bulletin board upon which is advertised what has been going on inside of us.

The author believes that there is no habit which will bring so much of value to the life as that of always carrying an optimistic, hopeful attitude of really *expecting* that things are going to turn out well with us and not ill, that we are going to succeed and not fail, are going to be happy and not miserable.

He points out that most people neutralize a large part of their efforts because their mental attitude does not correspond with their endeavor, so that although working for one thing, they are *really expecting* something else, and what we expect, we tend to get; that there is no philosophy or science by which a man can arrive at the success goal when he is facing the other way, when every step he takes is on the road to failure, when he talks like a failure, acts like a failure, for prosperity begins in the mind and is impossible while the mental attitude is hostile to it.

No one can become prosperous while he really expects or half expects to be always poor, for holding the poverty-thought keeps him in touch with poverty-producing conditions.

The author tries to show the man who has been groping blindly after a mysterious, misunderstood God, thought to dwell in some far-off realm, that God is right inside of him, nearer to him than hands and feet, closer than his heart-beat or breath, and that he literally lives, moves, and has his being in Him; that man is mighty or weak, successful or unsuccessful, harmonious or discordant, in proportion to the completeness of his conscious oneness with the Power that made him, heals his wounds and hurts, and sustains him every minute of his existence; that there is but one creative principle running through the universe, one life, one truth, one reality; that this power is divinely beneficent, that we are a necessary, inseparable part of this great principle-current which is running Godward.

The book teaches that everybody ought to be happier than the happiest of us are now; that our lives were intended to be infinitely richer and more abundant than at present; that we should have plenty of everything which is good for us; that the lack of anything which is really necessary and desirable does not fit the constitution of any right-living human being, and that we shorten our lives very materially through our own false thinking, our bad living, and our old-age convictions, and that to be happy and attain the highest efficiency, one *must* harmonize with the best, the highest thing in him.

December, 1910.   O. S. M.

CONTENTS

I. THE DIVINITY OF DESIRE

I. THE DIVINITY OF DESIRE

"And longing molds in clay what Life carves in the marble real."—LOWELL.

Your ambition, not your worded prayer, is your *real* creed.

"No joy for which thy hungering soul has panted,
    No hope it cherishes through waiting years,
But, if thou dost deserve it, shall be granted;
    For with each passionate wish the blessing
        nears.

"The thing thou cravest so waits in the distance,
    Wrapt in the silence unseen and dumb—
Essential to thy soul and thy existence,
    Live worthy of it, call, and it shall come."
                    —ELLA WHEELER WILCOX.

HATEVER the soul is taught to expect, that it will build."

Our heart longings, our soul aspirations, are something more than mere vaporings of the imagination or idle dreams. They are prophecies, predictions, couriers, forerunners of things which can become realities. They are indicators of our possibilities. They measure the height of our aim, the range of our efficiency.

3

What we yearn for, earnestly desire and strive to bring about, tends to become a reality. Our ideals are the foreshadowing outlines of realities behind them — the substance of the things hoped for.

The sculptor knows that his ideal is not a mere fantasy of his imagination, but that it is a prophecy, a foreshadowing of that which will carve itself in "marble real."

When we begin to desire a thing, to yearn for it with all our hearts, we begin to establish relationship with it in proportion to the strength and persistency of our longing and intelligent effort to realize it.

The trouble with us is that we live too much in the material side of life, and not enough in the ideal. We should learn to live mentally in the ideal which we wish to make real. If we want, for example, to keep young, we should live in the mental state of youth; to be beautiful, we should live more in the mental state of beauty.

The advantage of living in the ideal is that all imperfections, physical, mental, and moral, are eliminated. We can not see old age because old age is incompleteness, decrepitude, and these qualities can not exist in the ideal.

In the ideal, everything is youthful and

beautiful; there is no suggestion of decay, of ugliness. The habit of living in the ideal, therefore, helps us wonderfully because it gives a perpetual pattern of the perfection for which we are striving. It increases hope and faith in our ultimate perfection and divinity, because in our vision we see glimpses of the reality which we instinctively feel must sometime, somewhere, be ours.

The habit of thinking and asserting things as we would like to have them, or as they ought to be, and of stoutly claiming our wholeness or completeness — believing that we can not lack any good thing because we are one with the All Good,—supplies the pattern which the life-processes within us will reproduce. Keep constantly in your mind the ideal of the man or woman you would *like* to become. Hold the ideal of your efficiency and wholeness, and instantly strangle every disease image or suggestion of inferiority. Never allow yourself to dwell upon your weaknesses, deficiencies, or failures. Holding firmly the *ideal* and struggling vigorously to attain it will help you to realize it.

There is a tremendous power in the habit of expectancy, of believing that we shall realize our ambition; that our dreams will come true.

There is no more uplifting habit than that of bearing a hopeful attitude, of believing that things are going to turn out well and not ill; that we are going to succeed and not fail; that no matter what may or may not happen, we are going to be happy.

There is nothing else so helpful as the carrying of this optimistic, expectant attitude — the attitude which always looks for and expects the best, the highest, the happiest — and never allowing oneself to get into a pessimistic, discouraged mood.

Believe with all your heart that you will do what you were made to do. Never for an instant harbor a doubt of it. Drive it out of your mind if it seeks entrance. Entertain only the friend thoughts or ideals of the thing you are determined to achieve. Reject all thought enemies, all discouraging moods — everything which would even suggest failure or unhappiness.

It does not matter what you are trying to do or to be, always assume an expectant, hopeful, optimistic attitude regarding it. You will be surprised to see how you will grow in all your faculties, and how you will improve generally.

When the mind has once formed the habit of holding cheerful, happy, prosperous pictures, it will not be easy to form the opposite habit. If our children could only acquire this one habit, it would revolutionize our civilization very quickly and advance our life standards immeasurably. A mind so trained would always be in a condition to exercise its maximum power and overcome inharmony, unkindness and the hundred and one enemies of our peace, comfort, efficiency, and success.

The very habit of expecting that the future is full of good things for you, that you are going to be prosperous and happy, that you are going to have a fine family, a beautiful home, and are going to stand for something, is the best kind of capital with which to start life.

What we try persistently to express we tend to achieve, even though it may not seem likely or even possible. If we always try to express the ideal, the thing we would like to come true in our lives, whether it be robust health, a noble character, or a superb career, if we vizualize it as vividly as possible and try with all our might to realize it, it is much more likely to come to us than if we do not.

Many people allow their desires and longings to fade out. They do not realize that the very intensity and persistency of desire increases the power to realize their dreams. The constant effort to keep the desire alive increases the capacity to realize the vision.

It does not matter how improbable or how far away this realization may seem, or how dark the prospects may be, if we visualize them as best we can, as vividly as possible, hold tenaciously to them and vigorously struggle to attain them, they will gradually become actualized, realized in the life. But a desire, a longing without endeavor, a yearning abandoned or held indifferently will vanish without realization.

It is only when *desire crystallizes into resolve,* however, that it is effective. It is the desire coupled with the vigorous determination to realize it that produces the creative power. It is the yearning, the longing and striving together, that produce results.

We are constantly increasing or decreasing our efficiency by the quality and character of our thoughts, emotions, and ideals. If we could always hold the ideal of wholeness and think of ourselves as perfect beings, even as He is perfect, any tendency to disease anywhere would be neutralized by this restorative healing force.

Think and say only that which you wish to

become true. People who are always excusing themselves; constantly saying that they are tired, used up, played out, "all in," that they are all out of kilter somewhere; that they are always unfortunate, unlucky; that fate seems to be against them; that they are poor and always expect to be; that they have worked hard and tried to get ahead, but could not, little realize that they are etching these black pictures — enemies of their peace, happiness, and success, and the very things which they ought to wipe out of their minds forever — deeper and deeper into their consciousness, and are making it all the more certain that they will be realized in their lives. Never for an instant admit that you are sick, weak, or ill *unless you wish to ex--perience these conditions,* for the very thinking of them helps them to get a stronger hold upon you. We are all the products of our own thoughts. Whatever we concentrate upon, that we are. The daily habit of picturing oneself as a superb man sent to earth with a divine mission, and with the ability and the opportunity to deliver it grandly, gives a marvelous confidence, uplifting power and perpetual encouragement.

If you wish to improve yourself in any particular, visualize the quality as vividly and as tenaciously as possible and hold a superior ideal along the line of your ambition. Keep this persistently in the mind until you feel its uplift and realization in your life. Gradually the weak, imperfect man, which mistakes, sins and vicious living have made, will be replaced by the ideal man; your other, better God-self.

Every life follows its ideal; is colored by it; takes on its character; becomes like it. You can read a man's character if you know his ideal, for this always dominates his life.

Our ideals are great character-molders, and have a tremendous life-shaping influence. Our heart's habitual desire soon shows itself in the face; outpictures itself in the life. We can not long keep from the face that which habitually lives in our minds.

We develop the quality of the thought, emotion, ideal, or ambition which takes the strongest hold upon us. Therefore, you should let everything in you point toward superiority, nobility. Let there be an upward trend in your thinking. Resolve that you will never have anything to do with inferiority in your thoughts or your actions; that whatever you do shall bear the stamp of excellence.

This upreaching of the mind, this stretching of the mentality toward higher ideals and grander things, has an elevating, transforming influence which tends to lift the whole life to higher levels.

Human life is so constructed that we live largely upon hope; the faith that runs ahead and sees what the physical eye can not see.

Faith is the substance of things hoped for, *the outline of the image itself; the real substance, not merely a mental image.* There is something back of the faith, back of the hope, back of the heart yearnings; there is a reality to match our legitimate longing.

What we believe is coming to us is a tremendous creative motive. The dream of home, of prosperity, the expectancy of being a person of influence, of standing for something, of carrying weight in our community, — all these things are powerful creative motives.

Your whole thought current must be set in the direction of your life purpose. The great miracles of civilization are wrought by thought concentration. Live in the very soul of expectation of better things, in the conviction that something large, grand, and beautiful will await you if your efforts are intelligent, if your mind is kept in a creative condition and you struggle upward to your goal. Live in the conviction that you are eternally progressing, advancing toward something higher, better, *in every atom of your being.*

Many people have an idea that it is dangerous to indulge their dreaming faculties, their imagination, very much, for fear that in doing so they would become impracticable; but these faculties are just as sacred as any others we possess. They were given us for a divine purpose; so that we could get glimpses of intangible realities. They enable us to live in the ideal, even when we are compelled to work in the midst of a disagreeable or inhospitable environment.

Our dreaming capacity gives us a peep into the glorious realities that await us further on. It is the evidence of things possible to us.

Building air castles should no longer be looked upon as an idle, meaningless pastime. We first build our castles in our consciousness, picture them in detail in our ambition, before we put foundations under them and reality into them.

Dreaming is not always castle-building. Every real castle, every home, every building was an air castle first. Legitimate dreaming is creative; it is bringing into reality our desires; the things for which we long and hope. A building would be impossible without the plans of an architect; it must be created mentally. The architect sees behind the plans the building in all its perfection and beauty.

Whatever comes to us in life we create first in our mentality. As the building is a reality in all its details in the architect's mind before a stone or brick is laid, so we create mentally everything which later becomes a reality in our achievement.

Our visions are the plans of the possible life structure; but they will end in plans if we do not follow them up with a vigorous effort to make them real; just as the architect's plans will end in his drawings if they are not followed up and made real by the builder.

All men who have achieved great things have been dreamers, and what they have accomplished has been just in proportion to the vividness, the energy and persistency with which they visualized their ideals; held to their dreams and struggled to make them come true.

Do not give up your dream because it is apparently not being realized; because you can not see it coming true. Cling to your vision with all the tenacity you can muster. Keep it bright; do not let the bread-and-butter side of life cloud your ideal or dim it. Keep in an ambition-arousing atmosphere. Read the books which will stimulate your ambition. Get close to people who have done what you are trying to do, and try to absorb the secret of their success.

This mental visualizing of the ideal as vividly and as sharply as possible is the mental molding of the thing that will finally match your vision with its reality; that will make your dream come true.

Take a little time before retiring at night and get by yourself. Sit quietly and think and dream to your heart's content. Do not be afraid of your vision, or of your power to dream, for "without a vision the people perish." The faculty to dream was not given to mock you. There is a reality back of it. It is a divine gift intended to give you a glimpse of the grand things in store for you and to lift you out of the common into the uncommon; out of hampering, iron conditions into ideal ones, and to show you that these things can become realities in your life. *These glimpses into paradise are intended to keep us from getting discouraged by our failures and disappointments.*

I do not mean fanciful, ephemeral pipe dreaming, but real, legitimate desire and the sacred longings of the soul, which are given us as constant reminders that we can make our lives sublime; that no matter how disagreeable or unfriendly our surroundings may be, we can lift ourselves into the ideal conditions which we see in our vision.

There is a divinity behind our legitimate desires.

By the desires that have divinity in them, I do not refer to the things that we want but do not need; I do not refer to the desires that turn to dead-sea fruit on our lips or to ashes when eaten, but to the legitimate desires of the soul for the realization of those ideals, the longing for full, complete self-expression, for the time and opportunity for the weaving of the pattern shown us in the moment of our highest transfiguration.

"A man will remain a ragpicker as long as he has only a ragpicker's vision."

Our mental attitude, our heart's desire, is our perpetual prayer which Nature answers. She takes it for granted that we desire what our heart asks for — that what we want we are headed toward, and she helps us to it. People little realize that their desires are their perpetual prayers — not head prayers, but heart prayers — and that they are granted.

We are all conscious that there accompanies us through life a divine messenger, given to protect and direct us; a messenger who will answer all our interrogations. No one is mocked with the yearning for that which he has no ability to attain. If he holds the right mental attitude and struggles earnestly, honestly toward his goal, he will reach it, or at least approximate to it.

There is a tremendous creative, producing power in the perpetual focusing of the mind along the line of the desire, the ambition. It develops a marvelous power to attract, to create the thing we long for.

> "The thing we long for, that we are
> For one transcendent moment."

Our heart yearnings inspire our creative energies to do the things we long for. They are a constant tonic to our faculties and increase our ability, tending to make our dreams come true. Nature is a great one-price storekeeper who hands us out what we ask for if we pay the price. Our thoughts are like roots which reach out in every direction into the cosmic ocean of formless energy, and these thought-roots set in motion vibrations like themselves and attract the affinities of our desires and ambitions.

The bird does not have an instinct to fly

South in winter without a real South to match it; nor has the Creator given to us these heart yearnings, soul longings for a larger, completer life, for an opportunity for a full expression of our possibilities, nor the longing for immortality, without a reality to match them.

Everything in the vegetable world, our flowers, our fruits, come to their natural, flowering, fruitage and ripeness at the appointed time; the winter does not surprise the buds before they have had an opportunity to open up; the fruit is ready to drop off the trees before the snow comes; the growth is not stunted.

But if we should find when the winter came that all our fruit was still green, that the flowers were still in bud, and that instead of having developed they were cut off by the cold, we would realize that there was something at fault somewhere. And when we find that not one out of the hundreds of millions of human beings ever ripens into completeness, is never even half developed before cut off by death, we know here also something is wrong.

The windfalls which we see on every hand under the life tree are not normal. There is something wrong when men and women inheriting God-like qualities and capable of

infinite possibilities fall off the life tree before
they are half matured.

We feel the same protest that the windfall
apple feels against having its life blighted and
cut off before it has had time to ripen, to
develop its possibilities — the same protest that
the stalwart oak, still sleeping in possibility in
the acorn which is just beginning to sprout,
feels when it is ruthlessly torn from the soil.

Even the men most richly endowed with
ability, education, and opportunity, even the
giants of the race, after the completest life
possible, feel, as they stand on the edge of the
grave, that they are but human acorns with all
their possibilities still in them, just beginning
to sprout.

But it will not always be thus. All analogy
teaches that human life will eventually have an
opportunity for its complete blossoming, full
fruitage, *untrammeled self-expression.* There
will, if we follow our vision, be a time and an
opportunity for the blossoming of our desires,
the fulfilment of our ambition, the ripening of
our ideals, for they are the petals in the closed
bud which will find an opportunity, sometime,
somewhere, to open up and fling out their fragrance and beauty without blight or bruise to
strangle growth.

Our instinctive yearning for the time and opportunity for the complete, untrammeled unfoldment of our powers; our sense of the unfairness, the unfitness of being cut off before we have had half enough time in which to mature, to ripen — all these are greater evidences that there are realities to match these heart longings and soul yearnings than have ever been printed in any book.

We are beginning to see that there is material in every normal being to make the ideal perfect man, the perfect woman. If we could only mentally hold the perfect pattern, the perfect ideal persistently, so that it would become the dominant mental attitude, it would soon be woven into the life and we should become perfect human beings.

The divine injunction to be perfect, even as He is perfect, was not given man to mock him. The possibility of our waking in His likeness is literally true.

II. SUCCESS AND HAPPINESS ARE FOR *YOU*

II. SUCCESS AND HAPPINESS ARE FOR *YOU*

"If a man thinks sickness, poverty, and misfortune, he will meet them and claim them all eventually as his own. But he will not acknowledge the close relationship — he will deny his own children and declare they were sent to him by an evil fate."

"Poverty is the hell of which most modern Englishmen are most afraid."—CARLYLE.

"Poverty is the open-mouthed hell which yawns beneath civilization."—HENRY GEORGE.

Wealth is created mentally first.

The stream of plenty will not flow toward the stingy, parsimonious, doubting thought.

Holding the poverty thought keeps one in touch with poverty-producing conditions.

O man has a right, unless he can not help himself, to remain where he will be constantly subjected to the cramping, ambition-blighting influences and great temptations of poverty. His self-respect demands that he should get out of such an environment. It is his duty to put himself in a position of dignity and independ-

ence, where he will not be liable at any moment to be a burden to his friends in case of sickness or other emergencies, or where those depending on him may suffer.

Almost every wealthy man in this country will tell you that his greatest satisfaction and happiest days were when he was emerging from poverty into a competency; when he first felt the tonic from the swelling of his small savings towards the stream of fortune, and knew that want would no longer dog his steps. It was then he began to see ahead of him leisure, self-development, self-culture, or perhaps study and travel, and to feel that those whom he loved would be lifted from the clutches of poverty. Comforts were taking the place of stern necessities and blunting drudgery, and he realized that he had the power to lift himself above himself, that henceforth he would be of consequence in the world; that he might have pictures and music and books, luxuries for his home, and that his children might not have to struggle quite as hard for an education as he had. Then he first felt the power to give them and others a little start in the world; felt the tonic of growth, the little circle about him expanding into a larger sphere, broadening into a wider horizon.

There are plenty of evidences that we were made for grand things, sublime things; for abundance and not for poverty. *Lack and want do not fit man's divine nature.* The trouble with us is that we do not have half enough faith in the good that is in store for us. We do not dare fling out our whole soul's desire, to follow the leading of our divine hunger and ask without stint for the abundance that is our birthright. We ask little things, and we expect little things, pinching our desires and limiting our supply. Not daring to ask to the full of our soul's desire, we do not open our minds sufficiently to allow a great inflow of good things. Our mentality is so restricted, our self-expression so repressed, that we think in terms of stinginess and limitation. We do not fling out our soul's desire with that *abundant* faith which trusts *implicitly,* — and which receives accordingly.

The Power that made and sustains us gives liberally, abundantly, not stingily, to everybody and everything. There is no restriction, no limitation, no loss to anybody from His abundant giving.

We are not dealing with a Creator who is impoverished by granting our requests. It is His nature to give, to flood us with our heart's desires. He does not have less because we ask much. The rose does not ask the sun for only a tiny bit of its light and heat, for it is the sun's nature to throw it out to everything which will absorb it and drink it in. The candle loses nothing of its light by lighting another candle. We do not lose but increase our capacity for friendship by being friendly, by giving abundantly of our love.

One of the great secrets of life is to learn how to transfer the full current of divine force to ourselves, and how to use this force effectively. If man can find this law of divine transference, he will multiply his efficiency a millionfold, because he will then be a co-operator, co-creator with divinity, on a scale of which he has never before dreamed.

When we recognize that everything comes from the great Infinite Supply, and that it flows to us freely, when we get into perfect tune with the Infinite, when the brute has been educated out of us and the dross of dishonesty, selfishness, impurity, burned out of us, we shall see God without these scales, which make us blind to good; we shall see God, (good,) and we shall know good, for only the pure in heart *can* see God.

When unfairness, a desire to take advan-

tage of our brothers and sisters, is removed
from our lives, we shall get so close to God
that all of the good things in the universe will
flow to us spontaneously.   The trouble is that
we restrict the in-flow by wrong acts, wrong
thoughts.

Every vicious deed is an opaque veil, another
film over our eyes so that we can not see God
(good).   Every wrong step separates us from
Him.

When we learn the art of seeing opulently,
instead of stingily, when we learn to think
without limits, how not to cramp ourselves by
our limiting thought, we shall find that the
thing we are seeking is seeking us, and that it
will meet us half way.

John Burroughs beautifully expresses this in
his poem " Waiting ":

> "I rave no more 'gainst Time or Fate,
>   For lo, my own shall come to me.
>
> *   *   *
>
> "Asleep, awake, by night or day,
>   The friends I seek are seeking me.
>
> "What matter if I stand alone?
>   I wait with joy the coming years;
> My heart shall reap where it hath sown,
>   What is mine shall know my face.
>
> *   *   *

" Nor time, nor space, nor deep, nor high
Can keep my own away from me."

Do not be forever apologizing for your lack
of this or that. Every time you say that you
have nothing fit to wear, that you never have
things that other people have, that you never
go anywhere or do things that other people do,
you are simply etching the black picture deeper
and deeper. As long as you recite these unfortunate details and dwell upon your disagreeable experiences, your mentality will not attract
the thing you are after, will not bring that
which will remedy your hard conditions.

The mental attitude, the mental picturing,
must correspond with the reality we seek.

Prosperity begins in the mind, and is impossible with a mental attitude which is hostile
to it. We can not attract opulence mentally
by a poverty-stricken attitude which is driving
away what we long for. It is fatal to work
for one thing and to expect something else.
No matter how much one may long for prosperity, a miserable, poverty-stricken mental
attitude will close all the avenues to it. The
weaving of the web is bound to follow the
pattern. Opulence and prosperity can not
come in through poverty-thought and failure-

thought channels. They must be created mentally first. We must think prosperity before we can come to it.

How many take it for granted that there are plenty of good things in this world for others, comforts, luxuries, fine houses, good clothes, opportunity for travel, leisure, but not for them! They settle down into the conviction that these things do not belong to them, but are for those in a very different class.

But why are you in a different class? Simply because you *think* yourself into another class; think yourself into inferiority; because you place limits for yourself. You put up bars between yourself and plenty. You cut off abundance, make the law of supply inoperative for you, by shutting your mind to it. *And by what law can you expect to get what you believe you can not get? By what philosophy can you obtain the good things of the world when you are thoroughly convinced that they are not for you?*

The limitation is in ourselves, and not in the Creator. He wants His children to have all of the good things of the universe, because He has fashioned them for His own. If we do not take them, it is because we limit ourselves.

One of the greatest curses of the world is the

belief in the necessity of poverty. Most people have a strong conviction that some must necessarily be poor; that they were made to be poor. But there was no poverty, no want, no lack, in the Creator's plan for man. There need not be a poor person on the planet. The earth is full of resources which we have scarcely yet touched. We have been poor in the very midst of abundance, simply because of our own blighting limiting thought.

We are discovering that thoughts are things, that they are incorporated into the life and form part of the character, and that if we harbor the fear thought, the lack thought, if we are afraid of poverty, of coming to want, this poverty thought, fear thought incorporates itself in the very life texture and makes us the magnet to attract more poverty like itself.

It was not intended that we should have such a hard time getting a living, that we should just manage to squeeze along, to get together a few comforts, to spend about all of our time making a living instead of making a life. The life abundant, full, free, beautiful, was intended for us.

If we were absolutely normal, our living-getting would be a mere incident to our life-making. The great ambition of the race would be to develop a superb type of manhood, a beautiful, magnificent womanhood; man-making, man-building, instead of dollar-making, as now.

Resolve that you will turn your back on the poverty idea, and that you will vigorously expect prosperity; that you will hold tenaciously the thought of abundance, the opulent ideal, which is befitting your nature; that you will try to live in the realization of plenty, to actually feel rich, opulent. This will help you to attain what you long for. There is a creative force in intense desire.

The fact is, we live in our own worlds, we are creations of our own thought. Each builds his own world by his thought habit. He can surround himself with an atmosphere of abundance, or of lack; of plenty, or of want.

God's children were not made to grovel but to aspire; to look up, not down. They were not made to pinch along in poverty, but for larger, grander things. *Nothing is too good for the children of the Prince of Peace; nothing too beautiful for human beings; nothing too grand, too sublime, too magnificent for us to enjoy.* It is the poverty attitude, the narrowness of our thought that has limited us. If we had larger and grander conceptions of life, of our birthright; if, instead of whining, crawling, grumbling, sneaking and apologizing, we were to stand erect and claim our kingship, demand our rich inheritance, the inheritance which is an abundance of all that is good and beautiful and true, we should live far completer, fuller lives. We should not be so poverty-stricken but for the narrowness of our faith, the meanness of our conception of our birthright. There are plenty of evidences in man's construction and environment that he was made for infinitely grander and superber things than even the most fortunate of men now possess and enjoy.

Why should we not expect great, grand things, if we are made in God's image and are His children? We are heirs of all that is His, all that is beautiful and opulent in the universe. The very holding of the mind open toward all the good things of the world, expecting and appreciating them, will have everything to do with obtaining them.

There is something wrong when multitudes of the sons and daughters of the King of Kings, who have inherited all the good things of the universe, starve on the very shores of the stream of plenty, of opulence unspeakable, which flows past their very doors and which carries infinite supply.

Our circumstances in life, our financial condition, our poverty or our wealth, our friends or lack of them, our condition of harmony or discord, are all very largely the offspring of our thought. If our mental attitude has been one of want, if we have dwelt much upon lack, our environment will correspond. If our thinking has been open, generous, and broad, if we have thought in terms of abundance, prosperity, and have made a relative effort to realize these conditions, our environment will tend to correspond. Everything we get in life comes through the gateway of our thought and resembles its quality. If that is pinched, stingy, mean, what flows to us will be like it.

When we see people who have been for years in a poverty-stricken condition, unless there has been much ill health or very unusual misfortune, we know that somebody has been sinning, has been in a wrong, vicious, mental attitude. We should very likely find the head of the house a complainer against fate for the sparseness of his supply, the littleness of his inflow.

If you are dissatisfied with your condition, if you feel that life has been hard and the fates cruel, if you are a complainer of your lot, you will probably find that, whatever your condition may be, in your home or business or social *life, it is the legitimate offspring of your own thought, your own ideals, and that you have nobody to blame but yourself.*

Right thinking will produce right living; clean thinking, a clean life; and a prosperous, generous thought followed up by intelligent endeavor to make your thoughts and your ideals real will produce corresponding results.

If we learn to trust implicitly the Great Dispenser of All Good, the source of Infinite Supply, — the Power which brings seed time and harvest, the Power which feeds, which supplies, the Power which bids us take no thought for the morrow but consider the lilies how they grow, — and do our level best to improve our condition, we shall never know what want is.

There is nothing which the human race lacks so much as unquestioned, implicit confidence in the divine source of all supply. We ought to stand in the same relation to the Infinite Source as the child does to its parents. The child does not say, "I do not dare eat this food for fear that I may not get any more." It takes everything with absolute confidence and assurance that all its needs will be supplied, that there is plenty more where these things came from.

We do not have half good enough opinions of our possibilities; do not expect half enough of ourselves; we do not demand half enough, hence the meagerness, the stinginess of what we actually get. We do not demand the abundance which belongs to us, hence the leanness, the lack of fulness, the incompleteness of our lives. We do not demand *royally* enough. We are content with too little of the things worth while. *It was intended that we should live the abundant life,* that we should have plenty of everything that is good for us. No one was meant to live in poverty and wretchedness. *The lack of anything that is desirable is not natural to the constitution of any human being.*

Hold the thought that you are one with what you want, that you are in tune with it, so as to attract it; keep your mind vigorously concentrated upon it; never doubt your ability to get what you are after, and you will tend to get it.

Poverty is often a mental disease. If you are suffering from it, if you are a victim of it, you will be surprised to see how quickly your condition will improve when you change your mental attitude, and, instead of holding that miserable, shriveled, limited poverty image, turn about and face towards abundance and plenty, towards freedom and happiness.

Success comes through a perfectly scientific mental process. The man who becomes prosperous *believes* that he is going to be prosperous. He has faith in his ability to make money. He does not start out with his mind filled with doubts and fears, and all the time talk poverty and think poverty, walk like a pauper and dress like a pauper. He turns his face towards the thing he is trying for and is determined to get, and will not admit its opposite picture in his mind.

There are multitudes of poor people in this country who are *half satisfied to remain in poverty*, and who have ceased to make a desperate struggle to rise out of it. They may work hard, but they have lost the hope, the expectation of getting an independence.

Many people keep themselves poor by fear of poverty, allowing themselves to dwell upon the possibility of coming to want, of not having enough to live upon, by allowing themselves to dwell upon conditions of poverty.

The minds of the children in many families are saturated with the poverty thought; they hear it from morning till night. They see poverty-stricken conditions everywhere. They hear everybody talking limitation, lack. Everything about them suggests poverty.

Is it any wonder that children brought up in such an atmosphere repeat the poverty-stricken conditions of their parents and environment?

Did you ever think that your terror of poverty, your constant worry about making ends meet, your fear of that awful "rainy day," not only make you unhappy, but actually disqualify you from putting yourself in a better financial condition? You are thus simply adding to a load which is already too heavy for you.

No matter how black the outlook or how iron your environment, positively refuse to see anything that is unfavorable to you, any condition which tends to enslave you, and to keep you from expressing the *best* that is in you.

By what philosophy can you expect poverty thoughts, thoughts of lack and want, to produce prosperity? Your condition will correspond to your attitude and ideals. These form the patterns which are woven into the life web. If they are slovenly, poverty-stricken, your life condition will correspond.

Suppose a boy should try to become a lawyer without expecting to be admitted to the bar, or while believing that he would never amount to anything as a lawyer. He would fail. We tend to get what we expect, and if we expect nothing we get nothing. The stream can not rise higher than its fountainhead; no one can become prosperous when he expects or half expects to remain poor.

The man who is bound to win believes he is going to be prosperous; he starts out with the understanding with himself that he is going to be a successful man, a *winner* and not a loser. He does not say to himself all the time, "What's the use? The great business combinations are swallowing up the chances. Before long the multitude will have to work for the few. I do not believe I shall ever do anything more than make just a plain living in a very humble way. I shall never have a home and the things that other people have. I am destined to be poor and a nobody." A man will never get anywhere with such ideals.

Everybody ought to stand erect with face towards the sun of hope and prosperity. *Success and happiness are the inalienable rights of every human being.*

Every achievement has its origin in the mind, every structure is first a mental structure. The building is first completed in all its details in the architect's mind. The contractor merely puts the stones, the brick and other material around the idea. We are all architects.

Everything we do in life is preceded by some sort of a plan.

Some people would like to make money, but they keep their minds so pinched, so closed, that they are not in a condition to receive an abundance.

The man who expects prosperity *is constantly creating money in his mind, building his financial structure mentally.* There must be a mental picture of the prosperity first; the building around it is comparatively easy. It does not take as great a man to place the material around the idea as to create the idea, the mental picture. This is not idle dreaming, it is brain building, mental planning, mental constructon. Dogged imagination is often one of the most practical of faculties; the true dreamer is the believer, the achiever.

Let us put up a new image, a new ideal of plenty, of abundance. Have we not worshiped the God of poverty, of lack, of want, about long enough? Let us hold the thought that God is our great supply, that if we can keep in tune, in close touch with Him, so that we can feel our at-one-ness with Him, the great Source of all supply, abundance will flow to us and we shall never again know want.

The poor man is not always the one who has

little or no property, but the one who is poverty-stricken in his ideas, in his sympathies, in his power of appreciation, in sentiment; poverty-stricken in his opinion of himself, of his own destiny, and his ability to reach up; who commits *the crime of self-depreciation.*

It is *mental* penury that makes us poor.

How few people realize the possibility of mental achievement, the fact that everything is created by the mind first, before it becomes a material reality! If we were better mental builders we should be infinitely better material builders.

A Morgan or Rockefeller mentally creates conditions which make prosperity flow to him. The great achievers do comparatively little with their hands; they build with their thought, they are practical dreamers; their minds reach out into the infinite energy ocean and create and produce what the ideal, the ambition, calls for, just as the intelligence in the seed reproduces the tree plan coiled up within itself.

To be prosperous we must put ourselves in the prosperous attitude. We must think opulently, we must feel opulent in thought; we must exhale confidence and assurance in our very bearing and manner. Our mental attitude towards the thing we are striving for and the intelligent effort we put forth to realize it, will measure our attainment.

Parsimonious saving by cheese-paring efforts does not compare in effectiveness with the results of obeying the laws of opulence. We go in the direction of our concentration. If we concentrate upon poverty, if want and lack predominate in our thought, poverty-stricken conditions must result.

We must conquer inward mental poverty before we can conquer outward poverty.

Opulence in the larger sense in which we use it is everything that is good for us, abundance of all that is beautiful in life, uplifting and inspiring; abundance of all that is sublime and magnificent. Opulence is everything that will enrich the personality, the life, the experience.

True prosperity is the inward consciousness of spiritual opulence, wholeness, completeness; the consciousness of oneness with the very Source of abundance, Infinite Supply; the consciousness of possessing an abundance of all that is good for us, a wealth of personality of character that no disaster on land or sea could destroy.

III. WORKING FOR ONE THING AND EXPECTING SOMETHING ELSE

III. WORKING FOR ONE THING AND EXPECTING SOMETHING ELSE

Prosperity begins in the mind and is impossible while the mental attitude is hostile to it. It is fatal to work for one thing and to expect something else, because everything must be created mentally first and is bound to follow its mental pattern.

No one can become prosperous while he really expects or half expects to remain poor. We tend to get what we expect, and to expect nothing is to get nothing.

When every step you take is on the road to failure, how can you hope to arrive at the success goal?

It is facing the wrong way, toward the black, depressing, hopeless outlook, even though we may be working in the opposite direction, that kills the results of our effort.

OST people do not face life in the right way. They neutralize a large part of their effort because their mental attitude does not correspond with their endeavor, so that while working for one thing they are really expecting something else. They discourage, drive away. the very thing they are pursuing by holding the wrong

45

mental attitude towards it. They do not approach their work with that assurance of victory which attracts, which forces results, that determination and confidence which knows no defeat.

To be ambitious for wealth and yet always expecting to be poor, to be always doubting your ability to get what you long for, is like trying to reach East by traveling West. There is no philosophy which will help a man to succeed when he is always doubting his ability to do so, and thus attracting failure.

The man who would succeed must think success, must think upward. He must think progressively, creatively, constructively, inventively, and, above all, optimistically.

You will go in the direction in which you face. If you look towards poverty, towards lack, you will go that way. If, on the other hand, you turn squarely around and refuse to have anything to do with poverty, — to think it, — live it, or recognize it — you will then begin to make progress towards the goal of plenty.

Many of us work at cross purposes, because, while we would like to be rich, we believe in our hearts that we shall not become so, and our mental attitude, the pattern which the life processes follow, makes impossible the very thing we are working for. It is our penury attitude, our doubt and fear, our lack of self-faith and of faith in the all-abundant, infinite supply, that makes us poor.

You must not play the part of a poor man while you are exerting all your energy to make money. You must get into a prosperous mental attitude. As long as you carry about a poorhouse atmosphere with you, you will make a poorhouse impression; and that will never attract money.

There is a saying that every time the sheep bleats it loses a mouthful of hay. Every time you allow yourself to complain of your lot, to say, " I am poor; I can never do what others do; I shall never be rich; I have not the ability that others have; I am a failure; luck is against me," you are laying up so much trouble for yourself, making it all the more difficult to get rid of these enemies of your peace and happiness, for every time you think of them they will go a little deeper and deeper into your consciousness.

Thoughts are magnets which attract things like themselves. If your mind dwells upon poverty and disease, it will bring you poverty and disease. There is no possibility of your producing just the opposite of what you are holding in your mind, because your mental attitude is the pattern which is built into the life. Your accomplishments are achieved mentally first.

If you are always thinking of poor business, preparing for it, expecting it, are always complaining about the times and conditions and fearing that business is going to be bad, it *will* be bad — for you. No matter how hard you may work for success, if your thought is saturated with the fear of failure, it will kill your efforts, neutralize your endeavors, and make success impossible.

The terror of failure and the fear of coming to want and of possible humiliation keep multitudes of people from obtaining the very things they desire, by sapping their vitality and incapacitating them, through worry and anxiety, for the effective, creative work necessary to give them success.

The habit of looking at everything *constructively*, from the bright, hopeful side, the side of faith and assurance, instead of from the side of doubt and uncertainty; and the habit of believing that *the best* is going to happen, that the right *must* triumph; the faith that truth is bound finally to conquer error, that harmony and health are the reality and discord and disease the temporary absence of it—*this is the attitude of the optimist, which will ultimately reform the world.*

Optimism is a builder. It is to the individual what the sun is to vegetation. It is the sunshine of the mind, which constructs life, beauty, and growth in everything within its reach. Our mental faculties grow and thrive in it just as the plants and trees grow and thrive in the physical sunshine.

Pessimism is negative, it is the darkened dungeon which destroys vitality and strangles growth.

A fatal penalty awaits those who always look on the dark side of everything, who are always predicting evil and failure, who see only the seamy, disagreeable side of life. They draw upon themselves what they see, what they look for.

Nothing has power to attract things unlike itself. Everything radiates its own quality, and attracts things which are akin. If a man wants to be happy and wealthy, he must think the happy thought, hold the abundance thought, and not limit himself He who has a mortal dread of poverty generally gets it.

Stop thinking trouble if you want to attract its opposite. Stop thinking poverty if you want to attract wealth. Do not have anything to do with the things you have been fearing. They are fatal enemies to your advancement. Cut them off. Expel them from your mind. Forget them. Think the opposite thoughts just as persistently as you can, and you will be surprised to see how soon you will begin to attract the very things for which you long.

The mental attitude which we hold toward our work or our aim has everything to do with what we accomplish. If you go to your work with the attitude of a slave lashed to his task, and see in it only drudgery; if you work without hope, see no future in what you are doing beyond getting a bare living; if you see no light ahead, nothing but poverty, deprivation, and hard work all your life; if you think that you were destined to such a hard life, you can not expect to get anything else than that for which you look.

If, on the other hand, no matter how poor you may be to-day, you can see a better future; if you believe that some day you are going to rise out of humdrum work, that you are going to get up out of the basement of life into the drawing-room, where beauty, comfort, and joy await you; if your ambition is clean-cut, and you keep your eye steadily upon the goal which

you hope to reach and feel confident that you
have the ability to attain, you will accomplish
something worth while.

Keeping the faith that we shall some time do
the thing which we can not now see any
possible way of accomplishing, just holding
steadily the mental attitude, the belief that we
will accomplish it, that somehow, some way, it
will come to us, the clinging to our vision, gets
the mind into such a *creative* condition that it
becomes a magnet to draw the thing desired.

I have never known a man who believed in
himself and constantly affirmed his ability to do
what he undertook, who always kept his eye
constantly on his goal and struggled manfully
toward it, who did not make a success of life.
Aspiration becomes inspiration and then realization.

Try to keep your mind in an uplifting, up-
building attitude. Never allow yourself for an
instant to harbor a doubt that you are finally
going to accomplish what you undertake.

These doubts are treacherous, they destroy
your creative ability, neutralize ambition.
Constantly say to yourself, " I *must* have what
I need; it is my right and I am going to have
it."

There is a great cumulative, magnetic effect

in holding in your mind continually the thought that you were made for success, for health, for happiness, for usefulness, and that nothing in the world but yourself can keep you from it.

Form a habit of repeating this affirmation, this faith in your ultimate triumph; hold it *tenaciously, vigorously,* and after a while you will be surprised to find how the things come to you which you have so longed for, yearned for, and struggled towards.

I have seen a man, when all the results of half a lifetime of struggle and sacrifice had been swept away by financial disaster, when he had nothing left but his grit and determination, and a great family of hungry mouths to feed, who would not even for an instant admit that he would not get on his feet again. There was no use talking discouragement to that man! You might as well have tried to discourage a Napoleon. With clenched fists, and a determination which did not recognize defeat, he kept his eye resolutely on his goal and pushed on. In a few years he was on his feet again.

A man was not intended to be a puppet of circumstances, a slave to his environment, he was intended to *make* his environment, to *create* his condition.

Nothing comes to us without cause, and that

cause is mental. Our mental attitude creates our condition of success or failure. The result of our work will correspond with the nature of our thoughts, our habitual mental attitude. To produce, the mind must be kept in a positive, creative condition. A discordant, worrying, despondent, poverty-facing mental attitude will quickly render the mind negative, and will produce a troop of mental enemies that will effectually bar our way to success and happiness.

Our mental faculties are like servants. They give us exactly what we expect of them. If we trust them, if we depend upon them, they will give us their best. If we are afraid, they will be afraid.

Negative characters wait for things to happen. They have a feeling that somehow things are going to happen anyway, and that they can not do much to change them.

It is the positive constructive mental attitude that has accomplished all of the great things in the world. It is the creative, aggressive, pushing, stimulating power that is back of all achievement. A strong, vigorous character creates a condition that will force things to happen. Knowing that nothing will move of itself, he is always putting into operation forces that do things.

Many positive minds become negative by influences which destroy their self-confidence. They gradually lose faith in themselves. Perhaps this begins through the suggestion of incompetence from others, the suggestion that they do not know their business or are not equal to the position they hold. After a while, through this subtle suggestion, initiative is weakened; the victims do not undertake things with quite the same vigor as formerly; they gradually lose the power of quick decision, and soon fear to decide anything of importance. Their minds become vacillating. Thus, instead of the leaders they once were, they become followers.

What we vigorously resolve to do, believe in with all our heart, confidently expect, the mental forces tend to realize. The very intensity of expectation enlists the vigor of all the mental processes in trying to accomplish things. In other words, all the forces of the mind fall into line with our expectation and resolution.

Our expectancy, our determination to achieve the thing on which we have set our heart, forms a pattern, a working model, which the mind endeavors to reproduce in reality. It is the mental picture which is used as the model for the creative forces.

The man who is endowed with great expectancy and is determined to reach his goal, let what will stand in his way, by his very resolution gets rid of a lot of success enemies which trip up the weak and the irresolute.

There is a mysterious power in the Great Within of us which we can not explain, but which we all feel to be there, which tends to carry out our commands, our resolves, whatever they may be.

For example, if I persist in thinking and affirming that I am a nobody, that I am "a poor worm of the dust," that I am not as good as other people, I shall after a while begin really to believe this, and then a fatal acceptance will be registered in my subconsciousness, and the mental machinery will begin to reproduce the "nobody" pattern. If I radiate the thought of lack and of weakness, of inefficiency, the pattern will, of course, be woven into my life, and I shall express weakness, failure, poverty.

But, on the other hand, if I stoutly affirm that I am heir to all the good things in the universe and that they belong to me as my birthright, if I firmly declare my faith in my kingship and constantly assert that I am able to carry out superbly the great life purpose which is indicated in my bent, assert that power is mine, that health is mine, that I will have nothing to do with sickness, with weakness, with discord, I then make my mind so positive, so creative in its assertive attitude that, instead of destroying, it produces, instead of tearing down, it is building up for me the very thing for which I long.

Constructive thinking means health and prosperity. Our faculties were intended to be producers. Negative thinking means wretchedness, disease, suffering of all kinds. Constructive thought is man's protector, his saviour from all discord, poverty, disease. The people in the great failure army are negative thinkers, while those in the successful ranks are positive, constructive thinkers.

A vigorous, positive mental attitude is the best possible self-protection.

It is when we are negative that we say "yes" when if we had been positive — normal — we should have said "no." It is when we are negative, because our judgment is then defective, that we make bad bargains, poor investments, and do all sorts of foolish things. A negative mind is not in a position to take important steps. When we make our slips, our bad breaks and our unfortunate ventures and bad decisions, we are in a more or less discouraged, despondent, unbalanced state and are willing to do almost anything to get into a comfortable position, an attitude of assurance, anything to get rid of our fears and anxieties for the moment, for *when our minds are negative we are always cowards.*

While we are holding the positive thoughts and creating something, the negative, discouraging, sickly, hap-hazard thoughts do not get a chance to act upon us. It is in our non-producing moments that negatives, such as fear, worry, anxiety, hatred, and jealously get in their destructive work. While positive energy is busy creating something, we are not troubled with the destructive negative thoughts. It is negative people who are victims of "the blues," extreme mental depression.

The normal mind acts under law. The mental faculties will not give up their best unless they are marshaled by order. They respond cordially to system, but they rebel against slipshod methods. They are like soldiers. They must have a leader, a general, who enforces order, method.

The strength and persistency of our habitual thought-force measure our efficiency. The habitual thought-force in many people is so feeble and spasmodic that they can not focus their minds with sufficient vigor to accomplish much.

We can quickly tell the first time we meet a person whether his thought-force is constructive or weak, for every sentence he utters will partake of its quality.

It is the positive man who carries force. Some men are so positive, so constructive in their mentality, and carry such a power of conquest in their very presence, that the ordinary person instinctively follows. The world makes way for the robust character. He radiates power. His presence commands men. His very words carry the force of conviction.

People do not stop to analyze the reason for following a strong character. They instinctively obey superior mentality.

Some strangers we meet at once impress us as producers. They make a positive, aggressive impression; we instantly feel their qualities of leadership, feel that such persons will certainly succeed in their undertakings, that things must go their way. Other people make a weak, negative, indifferent impression upon us and we say they are failures; they do not blaze their own path. To make people feel your power, the positive faculties must dominate.

The art of all arts is to make one's life a perpetual victory, and this would not be difficult if we were properly trained. As it is, the mind is much of the time in a negative, non-creative condition; instead of causing things, acting, it is acted upon.

The graduate who goes into the world without training in what constitutes a positive and a negative mental attitude is liable to be ruined in a very short time. His doubts, fears, and lack of confidence, his timid and negative mental picture, the effect of his discouraged emotions, may utterly ruin his natural, positive, productive mind by making it negative, and this change may be accomplished wholly unconsciously.

It is of infinitely more value for a student or youth to know how to keep his mind up to its maximum creative power, by keeping it positive and avoiding everything which would make it negative and unproductive, than to learn all the Latin and Greek and philosophies in the world.

We often see college graduates fail because their minds have become negative and incapable of producing, creating. A few months of training the mental faculties and building up the weak, deficient ones by scientific right thinking would be worth more to them than a whole college course without it.

A positive thought develops constructiveness, and this is the most important of all mental qualities. If your mind is inclined to be negative, if you lack initiative, you can soon increase your constructiveness wonderfully by forming a habit of holding the positive, creative mental attitude towards *everything*. This is true even when you are enjoying recreation. It is always weakening to hold the negative thought. It is infinitely better, in fact, to hold the mind absolutely passive, for there is a great difference between the passive mind, the mind at rest, and the negative mind.

The mental loom weaves whatever pattern we give it. It reproduces the ideal, whether of discord or harmony, error or truth, courage or cowardice. The characteristics of the model are very quickly transferred to the subject.

You will find a tremendous help in constantly affirming that you are the person you wish to be; not that you hope to be, but that you actually *are* now. You will be surprised to see how quickly the part which you assume will be realized in your life, will be outpictured in your character.

What magnificent characters we could build

up by holding persistently in the mind that pattern which we wish woven into the life web, forming the health pattern, the pattern of wholeness, completeness, the pattern of the perfect man, the man God intended, the ideal man without spot or blemish!

What we need do is to keep the dominant qualities always in the ascendency, to discourage and kill the opposites, the enemies of all constructiveness.

The moment the building-up process — the chemical force in the soil, in the atmosphere, in the sunshine, in the rain — ceases to operate upon the plant, upon the fruit, upon the tree, the injurious elements set in, and decay and destruction are certain. So, the moment the building-up and creative principles in man cease to dominate, the moment he loses confidence in them, the tearing down and destructive elements begin their work.

The right mental attitude has a powerful influence in protecting the mind from the influence of bad suggestions. For instance, if you constantly deny the power of the evil which you are compelled to hear and see in a vicious environment this denial will have a great counteractive influence upon it.

On the other hand, if your attitude of mind

is that of responsiveness, receptiveness to the evil, if you encourage it, welcome it, enjoy it, it will have a very strong influence over you.

There is everything in keeping the mind saturated with one's aim until it becomes a life habit, in setting the life currents and all of the forces within us towards the goal of our ambition. This will after a while create a sort of tide which will tend to float things our way.

We must look out for the cross currents which bring discord — the thought currents of hatred, jealousy, envy, or unkind feelings towards others, the thought currents of revenge, of malice — for all these are enemies which sap our energies and handicap our progress.

Anything which produces discord cripples our effort. We must have harmony, peace of mind, freedom of thought, to get efficiency. In other words, all the thought currents must be creative instead of destructive. Currents of courage, confidence and determination — these are the electrical mental forces which bring success.

A great many people who are comparative failures would succeed if they could only keep the failure thought currents out of their mind. It is a great art to learn to clear the mind of rubbish, of fear, anxiety, and all of the things that hinder, and to fill it with vigorous, hopeful, uplifting thoughts. This is what puts the mind into the producing, creative attitude.

We radiate our mental attitude, our hopes or our fears; and our reputation and others' estimate of us have a great deal to do with our success. If others do not believe in us, if they think we are weak and timid because our mental radiation is negative, weak, and timid, we shall not be put forward for positions of importance or responsibility.

There is everything in radiating a confident, courageous, fearless impression; in carrying the confident air which accompanies the conquering habit.

People will think that if we are in the habit of conquering we are much more likely to win in the future than those who are in the habit of losing or who radiate an impression of weakness or inferiority.

In other words, it is nearly as important to make others believe in us as to believe in ourselves; and to do this we must carry a confident, victorious air.

There is a great difference between a man who lives like a victor, who goes about the world as a conqueror, and one who carries a submissive, vanquished air, who always acts as though he had been defeated in the great life race.

Compare the influence of a man like Theodore Roosevelt, who radiates force from every pore and gives an impression of great vigor and superb power, with that of a timid, retiring, self-effacing, apologizing man, who radiates weakness and shows inefficiency and the lack of a bold, vigorous nature. The world likes a man who has the bearing of a conqueror, who gives the impression that he is in the habit of winning and always expects to succeed.

It is the affirmation of force that carries the conviction, that gives the impression of power. If your attitude does not suggest power, you will never gain the reputation of being a positive force in the world.

Some people wonder that they amount to so little, that they cut so little figure and carry so little weight in their community. It is because they do not think and act like conquerors. They do not hold the constructive, victorious attitude; they give the impression of weaklings. No person can be magnetic until he learns the secret of radiating force. The positive character is magnetic; the negative repellant. Victors are always victorious mentally first.

There are people who give us the impression that they never expect to win out; all they desire is a chance to make a fairly comfortable living. They never expect anything but hard work. They start out with the idea that life at best is going to be a grind, when it should be a perpetual delight, a glory. The life properly lived is a continual growth, and the very knowledge of constant enlargement, the knowledge that we are pushing farther out on our mental horizon, should give a sense of satisfaction that nothing else can bestow. There is nothing that will take the place of a sense of victoriousness, a consciousness of perpetual winning.

One thing that should be instilled into a child's very being is that he was born for victory, born to conquer; that he is victory-organized, and not failure-organized, as many people seem to think they are. Nobody is organized for failure.

If children were trained always to hold the victorious attitude, to have great respect for themselves and unlimited faith in their possibilities, failure would be a very rare thing. The time will come when children will be taught to radiate force, to express vigor and hold the victorious attitude, and when this will be considered a most important part of their education and upbringing.

The mental life must be right before the physical can be harmonious. You must bear a healthy relation to your fellow men; you must stand right with your brothers before you can stand right with yourself or be truly healthy or happy.

If we would have the victorious attitude, we must eliminate all thoughts of jealousy, hatred, and revenge that may rankle in us, and cultivate that peace of mind and serenity of soul which is characteristic of the really great.

The whole philosophy of efficiency and happiness consists in the vigorous, consistent affirmation of the thing we are trying to be, and trying to do.

A young man starting out in life, anxious to succeed, must not say to himself, " I would like to succeed, but I do not believe I am really fitted for the part I have assumed. My profession or my vocation is so crowded, there are so many who can not get a decent living in this field, so many people out of employment, that I believe I have made a mistake; but I will work away the best I can. Perhaps I will come out somewhere." The young man who talks so, thinks so, does so, will come out *somewhere*. It will be at the " little end of the horn," out of pocket, out at the elbow, and out of a job.

The fact is, others estimate us by what we are, not by what we say. We must radiate our realities. We can *say* almost anything we wish, but people judge us by that intangible impression which our radiation makes upon them, because that is the reality of us. You can not keep your real thought, your real estimate of another from him, no matter how honeyed or flattering your words. If you have a grudge in your heart, if you are envious or jealous, if you are uncharitable or antagonistic, he will feel it. We may deceive another with our words, but we can not change our radiation unless we change our whole mental attitude towards him.

Think of a man trying to create wealth when his whole mental attitude, when his very face seems to say, " Keep away from me, Prosperity. Do not come near me. I would like to have you, but you were evidently not intended for me. My mission in life is a humble one, and, while I wish I could have the good things which the more fortunate enjoy, I really do not expect them."

Abundance can not get near a person holding such a mental attitude. The mind that fears and doubts repels prosperity.

Of course, men do not mean to drive opportunity, prosperity, abundance away from them; but they hold the mental attitude filled with doubts and fears, and, lacking faith and self-confidence, they repel without knowing it.

Many people go through life neither successes nor failures, neither rich nor poor. They live most of their lives balanced between lack and a little, because part of the time their minds are productive, creative, and part of the time negative — hence unproductive. So these people oscillate like a pendulum.

When they get a little courage, hope, enthusiasm, they produce a little, because their minds are creative. When they lose heart, become discouraged, are filled with doubts and fears, their minds become negative, uncreative, non-producing, and they slide back again to want.

The time will come when we shall be able to keep our minds in a productive, creative attitude all the time. Then our lives will be filled with an abundance of all that is good.

IV. EXPECT GREAT THINGS OF YOURSELF

IV. EXPECT GREAT THINGS OF YOUR-
SELF

Faith is an optimist because it sees the way out.
Doubt is a pessimist, can not see the way ahead and
fears because not conscious of being able to cope
with the uncertain.

Faith opens the door of ability and develops superiority.

The habit of expecting great things of ourselves
calls out the best that is in us.

Faith is the divine messenger sent to guide man,
blinded by doubt and sin.

HAT would be the probable
success of an animal tamer
who went into a cage with
ferocious wild beasts for the
first time full of fear, doubt,
uncertainty? What if he
said to himself, "I will
try to conquer these wild animals, but I really
do not believe I can do it. It is a pretty tough
proposition for a human being to try to conquer
a wild tiger from the jungles of Africa. There
may be men who can do it, but I doubt very
much whether *I* can."

If he should face wild beasts with such an attitude of weakness, doubt, and fear, he would very soon be torn to pieces. Bold courage is all that would save him. He must conquer with his eye first, and there must be a lot of winning, gritty stuff back of the eye, for the slightest show of fear would probably be fatal, the least indication of cowardice might cost him his life.

In fact, a man can not try with that determination which achieves unless he actually believes he is going to get what he is working for, or approximate to it.

How long will it take a youth to become a merchant who is always in doubt whether he will make much of a merchant anyway, and when he does not believe in his heart of hearts that he ever will be one? This is not the kind of mental attitude which makes anything worth while. The mind must lead; the pattern precedes the weaving of the web, the ideal must go ahead. *We always face in the direction of our faith.* It is what we *believe* we can do that we accomplish or tend to.

How long will it take a young man to make a fortune if he has not the slightest confidence that he will ever make money, if he starts out with the conviction that only a few can be rich, that most people are poor, and that he is probably one of the multitude?

How long would it take a boy to go through college who was always talking about the impossibility of his doing so, who was forever complaining that he had no chance, no money, nobody to help him, and that he never could do it without assistance?

How long would it take a youth out of work to get a good position if he should deny his ability to get one, and keep saying, " What is the use? "

I have known boys to resolve to become lawyers, physicians, or merchants with such a flimsy will, such a weak resolve, that they were daunted at the first difficulty. They were separated from their weak resolve before they were fairly started. It was the easiest thing in the world to turn them.

I have known other boys to decide upon their vocation with such **vigor** and **virility** that nothing could shake their decision, because it was a part of their very constitution.

If we analyze great achievements and the men who accomplish them, the most prominent quality in evidence is self-confidence. The man with absolute faith in his ability to do what he undertakes is the most likely to

succeed, even when such confidence seems to
outsiders audacious, if not foolhardy. It is not
alone the subjective effect of this belief in
themselves that enables such men to get results;
it is also largely the effect of that self-faith on
others. When a man feels a sense of mastery,
of having risen to his dominion, he talks confidence, radiates victory, and overcomes doubts
in others. Everybody believes he can do the
thing he undertakes. The world believes in
the conqueror, the man who carries victory in
his very appearance.

We believe in people who impress us with
their power, and they can not do this without
a strong self-faith. They can not do it when
their minds are full of doubts and fears. Some
men carry conquest in their very presence;
they win our confidence the first time we see
them. We believe in their power because they
radiate it.

In every kind of work and business we are
dependent on the belief of others that we can
make or carry out plans, can produce superior
goods, can manage employees, can do any of
the thousand things demanded by employers
or by the public. Life is too short, there is
not time enough, to allow minute investigation
of another's ability to achieve the thing he

assumes to be able to do; therefore, the world accepts very largely a man's own estimate of himself until he forfeits its confidence. A physician does not have to prove to each patient that he has followed certain courses and passed certain examinations. If a young man hangs out his law shingle, the world will take it for granted that he is fitted for his profession until he proves otherwise.

You will notice in a group of boys or young men who are friends or schoolmates, with similar ability and education, that one will step out boldly and advance rapidly, while the others are *waiting for somebody to discover them.* The world is too busy to hunt for merit. It takes it for granted that you can do what you claim you can, until you show your inability.

To acknowledge lack of ability, to give way to a temporary doubt, is to give failure so much advantage. We should never allow self-faith to waver for a moment, no matter how dark the way may seem. Nothing will destroy the confidence of others so quickly as a doubt in our own minds. Many people fail because they radiate their discouraged moods and project them into the minds of those about them.

If you are always putting a low rating on

yourself, marking yourself down, you may be sure that others will not take the trouble to mark you up. They will not take pains to see if you have not rated yourself too low.

I never knew a man who had a small, belittling estimate of himself to do a great thing. We can never get more out of ourselves than we expect. If you expect large things from yourself, and demand them, if you hold the large mental attitude toward your work, you will get much bigger results than if you depreciate yourself and look only for little results.

If you think you are peculiar, that you are not like other people, that you are different and can not achieve what they do, — if you harbor these impressions, you are not in a position to overcome what you regard as a handicap. The consciousness of possessing such qualities keeps you from being yourself.

People who are constantly depreciating themselves, effacing themselves, who believe that they are miserable worms of the dust and that they never will amount to anything of consequence, make a corresponding impression upon others, for they look as they feel.

Your own estimate of yourself, of your ability, your standing, the weight you carry, and of the figure you cut in the world, will be out-pictured in your appearance, in your manner.

If you feel very ordinary you will appear very ordinary. If you do not respect yourself you will show it in your face. If you feel poor, if you have a skim-milk opinion of yourself, you may be sure that nothing very rich will manifest itself in you. Whatever qualities you attribute to yourself, you will manifest in the impression you make upon others.

On the other hand, if you always contemplate the very qualities which you long to possess, they will gradually become yours, and you will express them in your face and manner. You must feel grand to look grand. There must be superiority in your thought before it can be expressed in your face and your bearing.

Confidence is the very basis of all achievement. There is a tremendous power in the conviction that we can do a thing.

The man who has great faith in himself is relieved from a great many uncertainties as to whether he is in his right place, from doubts as to his ability, and from fears regarding his future.

In others words, the man who is faith-protected is released from a great many worries and anxieties which handicap those who are not. He has freedom of faculty and freedom of action, both of which are necessary for the greatest efficiency.

Freedom is essential to achievement. No one can do his greatest work when his mind is cramped with worry, anxiety, fear, or uncertainty, any more than he can do his best physical work with his body in a cramped position. Absolute freedom is imperative for the best brain work. Uncertainty and doubt are great enemies of that concentration which is the secret of all effectiveness.

Confidence has ever been the great foundation stone. It has performed miracles in every line of endeavor.

Who can ever estimate the marvelous influence of faith in the great achievements of men, that kind of faith which annihilates obstacles, which removes mountains of difficulties?

We are constantly reminded in the Bible that it was through faith that Abraham, Moses, and all the great characters were able to perform miracles and do such marvelous things. There is no other one thing that is emphasized so much throughout the Bible as the importance of faith. "According to thy faith be it unto thee" is reiterated throughout the Scriptures.

We are told that it is faith that doubles one's power and multiplies one's ability, and that without it we can do nothing. How quickly a strong man is stripped of his power the moment he loses confidence in himself or his ability!

Faith is the great connecting link between the objective and the subjective states. It is our faith that enters the Great Within of us, the holy of holy of our lives, and touches the divine. Faith opens the door of the true source of life, and it is through faith that we touch Infinite Power.

Our life is grand or ordinary, large or small, in proportion to the insight and strength of our faith.

Many people do not trust their faith, because they do not know what it is. They confuse it with fancy or imagination, but it is the voice of a Power Within in touch with Omnipotence. It is a spiritual faculty which does not guess or think or doubt, but which *knows,* for it sees the way out, which the other faculties can not see. It is knowledge just as real as the knowledge which we gain through the senses.

Faith is a great elevator of character, and

has a wonderful influence on the ideals. It lifts us to the heights and gives us glimpses of the promised land. It is "the light of truth and wisdom."

It is criminal to destroy a child's faith in himself by telling him that he will never amount to anything, that he is a nobody, that he can not do what others do.

Parents and teachers little realize how extremely sensitive young minds are, and how powerfully influenced they are by anything which suggests their inferiority or their incompetence.

The suggestion of inferiority has caused more individual wretchedness, tragedies, and failures in life than anything else.

Dr. Luther H. Gulick, the physical director of the schools of New York City, says that there is a great army of boys and girls who drop out of our public schools because of their failure to pass examination, the reason for which has often been traced to impaired eyesight, defective hearing, bad teeth, or to the lack of proper nourishment. But the children do not appreciate these things and often do not know why they are inefficient, and they become morose, depressed, and humiliated because of their failure, and sometimes their minds become completely unbalanced.

Every year a number of them actually commit suicide.

Even the best race horse could not win a prize if its confidence were destroyed. This is one of the things the trainers are always careful to retain, for the animal's confidence that he can win is a very great factor in victory.

It is faith that unlocks our power and enables us to use our ability. It has been the great miracle-worker of the ages. Whatever will increase your confidence in yourself increases your power.

Men who do great things in this world are always characterized by large faith in themselves, faith in their power, faith in the future of the race, while the men who do little things are characterized by their lack of faith, which makes them timid.

That one quality of holding persistently the faith in themselves, and never allowing anything to weaken the belief that somehow they would accomplish what they undertook, has been the underlying principle of all great achievers. The great majority of men and women who have given civilization a great uplift started poor, and for many dark years saw no hope of accomplishing their ambition; but they kept on working and believing that some-how a way would be opened. Think of what this attitude of hopefulness and faith has done for the world's great inventors! How most of them plodded on through many years of dry, dreary drudgery before the light came! And the light probably would never have come but for their faith, hope, and persistent endeavor.

We are enjoying to-day thousands of bless-ings, comforts, and conveniences which have been bequeathed us by those resolute souls who were obliged often to turn a deaf ear to the pleadings of those they loved best, as they struggled on amid want and woe for many years without the sympathy or confidence of those nearest them.

Faith is the best substitute for genius; in fact, it is closely allied to genius.

Faith is the great leader in every achieve-ment. It shows the path which leads the way to our possibilities. Faith is the faculty or in-stinct which knows, because it sees the possi-bilities within; it does not hesitate to urge us to undertake great things, because it sees re-serves in us capable of accomplishing them.

No one has ever yet been able to make a satisfactory explanation of the philosophy of faith. What is that which will hold a man to his task, keep up his courage and hope under the most trying, heartrending conditions, which will enable him to endure with fortitude, even cheerfulness, all sorts of suffering, the pangs of poverty, and which will sustain and re-assure him, after his last dollar has gone, when friends and even his family and those he loves best misunderstand him, or do not believe in him? What is it that sustains and enheartens him so that he endures what would kill him a hundred times if he were without it? The world stands in wonder before the heroes who apparently lose everything in the world but their faith in what they had set their hearts upon.

Faith always takes the first step forward. It is a soul sense, a spiritual foresight, which peers far beyond the physical eye's vision, a courier which leads the way, opens the closed door, sees beyond the obstacles, and points to the path which the less spiritual faculties could not see.

It is a superb faith greater than any obstacle that has made the great discoveries, that has been the great inventor, the great engineer, the great achiever in every line of human endeavor.

There is little fear for the future of the

young man who has a deep-seated faith in himself. Self-faith has ever been more than a match for difficulties. It has been the poor man's friend, his best capital. Men with no assets but colossal faith in themselves have accomplished wonders, when capital without self-faith has failed.

If you believe in yourself, you will be much more likely to do the larger things you are capable of than if you were to hold the self-depreciatory, lack-of-confidence attitude.

If we could put a measuring line around a man's faith, it would give a pretty good estimate of his possibilities. No man ever does a great thing with little faith. If his faith is weak, his efforts will be weak.

If you admit that you are full of flaws, that you are a blunderer, always unlucky, that you can never do things as other people do, how can you possibly expect other than that your acts will follow the convictions which you are constantly emphasizing?

If you go about with an apologetic air as though you would *pick up anything that anybody else dropped and be glad to get it,* but that you do not expect much of yourself; as though you do not believe that the grand things, the good things of the world are intended for you, you will pass for a very small man. And it is a fact that others' estimate of us has a great deal to do with our place in life and what we achieve. We can not get away from it.

I know a man who creeps into a board meeting where he is a director as though he were a nobody, entirely unworthy of his position, and he wonders why he is a mere cipher on the board, why he carries so little weight with other members, why he is hardly ever deferred to.

He does not realize that he has lived with himself a good while and by this time ought to know himself better than others who see him only occasionally and naturally take him at his own rating. If he labels himself all over with the tags of inferiority, if he walks and talks and acts like a nobody and gives the impression that he does not think much of himself anyway, how can he expect others to do for him what he will not do for himself?

If we had a larger conception of our possibilities, a larger faith in ourselves, we should accomplish infinitely more. And if only we better understood our divinity we should have this larger faith. We are crippled by the old doctrine that man is by nature depraved.

There is no inferiority or depravity about the man that God made. The only inferiority in us is what we put into ourselves. What God made is perfect. The trouble is that most of us are but a burlesque of the man God patterned, intended. We think ourselves into smallness, into inferiority by thinking downward. We ought to think upward, if we would reach the heights where superiority dwells.

One of the most unfortunate phases of ancient theology is in the idea of the debasement of man, that he has fallen from his grand original estate. The truth is that he has always been advancing as a race, always improving, but his progress has been greatly hampered by this belittling idea. The man God made never fell. It is only the sin-made man that has fallen. It is only his inferior way of looking at himself, his criminal self-depreciation, that has crippled and deteriorated him.

The old theology taught us to belittle ourselves. There was a begging element in it. There is nothing in the Bible to indicate that man was to prostrate himself before his Maker like a sneak or a slave. There is nothing in such self-depreciation but demoralization. There is too much of the cringing, crawling spirit in our attitude; there is too much of the prostration, too much of the knee-idea, in our theology. Man was not made to bow in humiliation and shame, but to assert his divinity. He was made erect so that he could stand up and look anything and everything in the face, even his Maker, for he was made in His image.

If man is a prince, if he has royal blood in his veins, if he has inherited the divine moral attributes, he should claim his birthright boldly, manfully, with dignity and assurance.

The trouble with us is that we do not keep our good qualities sufficiently in sight; we do not think half well enough of ourselves. If we did, we would have a much better expression, would present a divine appearance.

It makes all the difference in the world to us whether we go through life as conquerors, whether we go about among men as though we believed we amounted to something, with a strong, vigorous, self-confident, victorious air, or whether we go about with an apologetic, self-effacing, get-out-of-other-people's-way attitude.

Is there any reason why we should go through the world whining, tagging at somebody else's heels trailing, imitating, copying somebody else, afraid to call our souls our own? Hold up your head, and learn to think well of yourself; have a good opinion of yourself, and your ability to do what you undertake. If you do not, nobody else will.

Much of the poverty and lack of social position among people of the working class in this country to-day are due to their own sense of inferiority. Instead of standing up in an attitude of manliness and independence they take it for granted that they are inferior. If there is anything a level-headed, spirited employer despises it is a truckling, pandering, apologizing attitude in his employees. He likes to have those about him approach him on the equality of manhood. He instinctively despises those who bow and scrape. He can never respect the leave-it-all-to-you employee. He likes the one who stands up for his rights, and who makes him feel that he is a man and expects to be treated as a man.

Whether we realize it or not, we are never stronger than our faith, we never undertake anything greater than our self-confidence dictates.

The habit of exercising self-faith, of feeling conscious of possessing greater ability and power than we are using, has a tremendous ex-

tending, enlarging, unfolding influence upon
our mental faculties. So undeveloped are our
latent sources of power that our self-faith is
rarely so great as the ability back of it would
warrant.

As a rule a man's greatest deficiency is that
of self-faith.

The majority of people are many times
weaker in confidence than any other faculty.
A large percentage of those who are failures
could have succeeded if this one quality had
been properly trained and strengthened in their
youth.

Take a timid, shy, sensitive, shrinking
individual, and teach him to believe in himself,
teach him that he has great possibilities, that he
can make himself a man who will stand for
something in his community. Train him in
self-faith until this quality becomes strong and
robust, and it will not only increase his courage, but strengthen all his other mental qualities as well.

The life processes are all the time reproduc-
ing the mental picture, the opinion we have
of ourselves. No man can be greater than his
estimate of himself at the moment. If a genius
were convinced that he were a pygmy, he would
only produce the results of a pygmy until he

enlarged his estimate of himself. It does not matter how great or grand one's general ability may be, his self-estimate will determine the results of his efforts. A one-talent man with an overmastering self-faith often accomplishes infinitely more than a ten-talent man who does not believe in himself.

I know of no greater self-protection from all that is low, ordinary, and inferior than the cultivation of a lofty, grand estimate of one-self and one's possibilities. All the forces within you will then work together to help you realize your ideals, for the life always follows the aim; we always take the direction of the life purpose.

Hold up-building, ennobling, sublime pictures of yourself and your divine possibilities. If you persist in this constant struggle to measure up to higher and higher ideals, loftier and loftier standards, the life processes within you will help you to realize them.

It does not matter how strong most of our mental faculties are, if they are not led by a vigorous faith. Faith puts all the other faculties to work. Its influence upon the mental faculties is very bracing, while that of doubt and fear is demoralizing, deteriorating. There is nothing that will so brace a man up, will so buttress and reinforce his weaker faculties, as a robust self-faith, faith in himself, faith in everybody and in everything, faith that there is a great, magnificent force in civilization, in the affairs of man, a current which runs Godward; that there is a divinely beneficent purpose running through the universe.

Faith powerfully encourages all the other faculties, and courage is a tremendous force in one's life. The greater our faith, the closer, the nearer, becomes our oneness with the universal life, universal power.

Doubt is a great paralyzer of efficiency. A man must believe that he can do a thing before he can do it. He can do little while he doubts. A man whose purpose is backed up by a superb faith and a lofty ambition, so that he finds neither comfort, rest, nor satisfaction until he is successful, will perform miracles, no matter what circumstances may conspire to hinder him.

The very intensity of your longing to do a certain thing is an additional proof that you have the ability to do it, and the constant affirmation that you can and will do it makes the achievement all the more certain. What you dream you can do, think you can do or believe you can do, you will do.

Faith is the bed rock upon which all other foundation stones in every great character rest. Thus the man who has an invincible faith in his mission, an unconquerable faith in himself and in his God, has power in the world.

We believe in a man with great faith, no matter whether he agrees with us or not, because faith represents force, stability, character. We believe in a man in proportion to his immovableness from principle, the fixity of his faith in his mission. The man who is loosely attached to his life work, who can be easily turned aside from his life purpose, is not much of a man.

Most successful men I have known had the habit of expecting things to turn out right. No matter how black or discouraging the outlook, they held tenaciously to their faith in the final outcome. This habit of holding an expectant attitude in some mysterious way unknown to us attracts the thing we long for, just as though our own were always seeking us when we were seeking it.

Our faculties work under orders, and they tend to do or produce what is expected of them. If we expect a great deal, make a great demand of them, and insist on their helping us to carry out our ambition, they fall into line and proceed to help us. If, on the other hand, we do not have confidence enough to make a vigorous demand, a strenuous effort, if we waver or are in doubt, our faculties will lose their courage, and their effort will be perfunctory, will lack efficiency.

The mental faculties are very dependent upon the courage and confidence of their leader. They will give up all they have to the dominating will which governs them. But if their leader wavers, hesitates, they waver and hesitate also. Self-confidence is not a separate quality any more than courage is. It is a part of all the mental faculties, and when it is weak there is a corresponding lack of their efficiency, and *vice versa.*

I know of no other habit which would bring so much of value to our lives as that of always expecting that the best will happen to us instead of the worst, of taking it for granted that we are going to win out in whatever we undertake.

Many people queer their success at the very outset by expecting that they are going to fail, thinking that the chances are against them. In other words, their mental attitude is not favorable to the success which they are after. It sometimes even attracts failure. Success is achieved mentally first. If the mental attitude is one of doubt, the results will correspond. There must be persistent faith, continuous confidence, in order to win. A wavering, doubting mind brings wavering, doubting results.

There are many people who are habitually successful. Everything they touch seems to turn out well. They start out with the expectation of succeeding, with full, complete confidence that they are going to win, and they do.

One reason why so many fail or at best plod along in mediocrity is because they see so many obstacles and difficulties looming up so threateningly that they lose heart and are in a discouraged condition much of the time. This mental attitude is fatal to achievement, for it makes the mind negative, non-creative. It is confidence and hope that call out the faculties and multiply their creative, producing power.

The habit of dwelling on difficulties and magnifying them weakens the character and paralyzes the initiative in such a way as to hinder one from ever daring to undertake great things. The man who sees the obstacles more clearly than anything else is not the man to attempt or do any great thing. The man who does things is the man who sees the end and defies the obstacles.

If the Alps had looked so formidable to Napoleon as they did to his advisers and other people, he would never have crossed them in midwinter.

It is the man who persists in seeing his ideal, who ignores obstacles, absolutely refuses to see failure; who clings to his confidence in victory, success, that wins out.

Great things are done under the stress of an over-powering conviction of one's ability to do what he undertakes. There is irresistible force in a powerful affirmative expressed with unflinching determination. One might as well have tried to move Gibraltar itself as to have attempted to turn Napoleon from his course or change his decision when he had given his ultimatum.

Faith was given to support us, to reassure us when we can not see light ahead, or solve our problems. It is to the individual what the compass is to the mariner in the storms. He feels the same assurance when he can not see anything ahead, because his compass points true to his destination.

It is infinitely easier to force a huge shell through the steel plates of a ship when projected with lightning speed from the cannon than to push it through slowly. So the world makes way for force and persistency, for the man who knows which way he is going and who projects himself with vigor. The things which are always tripping the hesitating, the doubtful, the weak man, get out of the way of the vigorous, positive, decided man. Difficulties are great or small in proportion as you are great or small. They loom up like mountains to one man and dwindle to mole hills to another. It is only the little man, the weak man who is afraid of hard things, who shrinks before obstacles, because he lacks the momentum to force them out of his way.

Do not be afraid of taking responsibilities. Make up your mind that you will assume any responsibility which comes to you along the line of your legitimate career and that you will bear it a little better than anybody else ever before has. There is no greater mistake in the world than that of postponing present responsibility thinking that we will be better prepared to assume it later. It is accepting these positions as they come to us that gives us the preparation; for we can do nothing of importance easily, effectively, until we have done it so many times that it becomes a habit. On the very resolution to do the thing which is best for you — no matter how disagreeable, no matter how humiliating, no matter how much you may suffer from sensitiveness or a feeling of unpreparedness — depends the development of your manhood.

Do not be afraid to demand great things of yourself. Powers which you never dreamed you possessed will leap to your assistance. "Trust thyself. Every heart vibrates to that iron string."

The habit of expecting great things of ourselves calls out the best in us. It tends to awaken forces which but for the greater demand, the higher call, would remain latent.

You will find a stimulating effect in always considering yourself as lucky or fortunate. It is a great thing to form a habit of expecting good from every experience in life. Just think what it means to have everybody think you are lucky and expect that what you undertake will turn out well!

The reputation of always being successful in undertakings has been of great advantage to Theodore Roosevelt. He has the reputation of being a success organizer, and great things are expected of him. No matter what he goes into, or what he takes up, he seems to expect that he is going to win out. Thus, instead of getting a pulling back, hindering effect from people's doubts and fears, he has the tonic effect of their optimistic expectancy. He inspires good will which is contagious, because he carries such a positive, vigorous assurance. He believes that he was made to do things, to achieve, and this self-faith has inspired the confidence of a whole nation and earned for him a splendid reputation which wins half his battles and practically insures at the very outset the success of whatever he undertakes.

Many people never seem to come to themselves until they have received a great humiliating defeat. This seems to touch a spring deep in their nature, setting free dynamic forces which enable them to do marvels. When a man who has got the right stuff in him has made a slip and feels that he is down and out, when he sees those that know him regarding him as a failure, calling him a " has been," he makes a resolve to redeem himself from the disgrace, and every red blood corpuscle in him helps him to make good. There is something in the man whose very bearing and reputation seem to say, " When I meet my next Waterloo I shall be a Wellington, not a Napoleon."

CONFESSIONS OF A LUNKHEAD

I'm a lunkhead, an' I know it; 'tain't no use to
squirm an' talk,
I'm a gump an' I'm a lunkhead, I'm a lummux, I'm
a gawk.
An' I make this interduction so thet all you folks
can see
An' understan' the natur' of the critter thet I be.

Wall, thet's the kind er thing I be; but in our
neighborhood
Lived young Joe Craig, an' young Jim Stump, an'
Hiram Underwood.
We growed like corn in the same hill, jest like
four sep'rit stalks;
For they wuz lunkheads, jest like me, an' lummuxes
an' gawks.

Now, I knew I wuz a lunkhead; but them fellers
didn't know,
Thought they wuz bigges' punkins an' the purtiest
in the row.
An' I, I uster laff an' say, " Them lunkhead chaps
will see
W'en they go out into the worl' w'at gawky things
they be."

Joe Craig, he wuz a lunkhead, but it didn't get
through his pate;
I guess you've all heerd tell of him — he's gov'nor
of the State!
Jim Stump, he blundered off to war — a most un-
common gump —
Didn't know enough to know it—an' he come home
General Stump.

Then Hiram Underwood went off, the bigges' gawk
    of all,
We thought him hardly bright enough to share in
    Adam's fall;
But he tried the railroad biz'ness, an' he allus
    grabbed his share,—
Now this gawk who didn't know it is a fifty
    millionaire.

An' often out here hoein' I set down atween the
    stalks,
Thinkin' how we four together all were lummuxes
    an' gawks,
All were gumps, an' all were lunkheads, only they
    didn't know, yer see;
An' I ask, "If I hadn't known it, where in nature
    would I be?"

For I stayed to home an' rastled in the cornfiel',
    like a chump,
Coz I knew I wuz a lunkhead, an' a lummux, an' a
    gump;
But if only I hadn't known it, like them other
    fellers there,
To-day I might be settin' in the presidential chair.

We all are lunkheads — don't git mad — an' lum-
    muxes an' gawks;
But us poor chaps who know we be — we walk in
    humble walks.
So, I say to all good lunkheads, Keep yer own
    selves in the dark;
Don't own or reckernize the fact, an' you will make
    yer mark.—SAM WALTER FOSS.

V.   SELF-ENCOURAGEMENT BY SELF-SUGGESTION

V. SELF-ENCOURAGEMENT BY SELF-SUGGESTION

In proportion as you increase your confidence in yourself by the affirmation of what you wish to be, your ability will increase.

He only is beaten who admits it.

Hold the thought of superiority and you will become superior.

ANY people of real ability do little things all their lives because they are the victims of discouraging self-suggestions. Whenever they attempt to do anything, they allow their minds to dwell on the possibility of failure, and they picture the consequent humiliation of it all until they cripple their powers of initiative.

One of the worst things that can ever happen to a person is to get it into his head that he was born unlucky and that the Fates are against him. There are no Fates, outside of our own mentality. We are our own Fates. We control our own destiny.

In every town where people are complaining that their environment is against them and that there are no opportunities, others under the same conditions manage to succeed and make themselves felt in the world.

What can you do for a man who thinks he was born for failure? It is as impossible for success to come from the failure thought as for roses to come from thistle seeds. When one is greatly worried about failure or poverty, when he thinks much about it, he impresses his sub-consciousness with the very idea of failure, and develops unfavorable conditions. In other words, his thought, his mental attitude, is making impossible the very thing he is trying to accomplish.

We attribute much to luck or a cruel fate which belongs to our thought. We see people right alongside of us apparently with no greater ability wonderfully prosperous, while we are very indifferently so or perhaps total failures, and we are apt to think that there is a mysterious destiny which helps them, and that there is something outside of ourselves which keeps us back. But the probabilities are that the fault is in our thought, in our attitude of mind.

The trouble with us is that we do not half know how to jack ourselves up, so to speak. We are not severe enough with ourselves, not exacting enough; do not demand enough of ourselves. We should see ourselves in a much grander light; should think of ourselves as superb beings with infinite, divine possibilities. Don't be afraid of thinking too highly of yourself, for if the Creator made you, you must have inherited divine, omnipotent possibilities, you must partake of His qualities.

There is a powerful magic, a real creative force, in trying to become that which you wish to be, in assuming the character you would be like, assuming the qualities you would attain.

You want health. Never allow yourself to think that anything else will come to you. Assume the health attitude, think health, talk it. Say to yourself that it is your birthright.

The same is true in regard to prosperity. Do not allow yourself to think that anything else can come to you but prosperity. Assume the prosperity attitude, thought, manner. Act like a prosperous, progressive man, dress like one, *think* like one. Be sure that your mental picture, your mental attitude, is the pattern of that which you would like to be a reality.

If you wish to be brave, courageous, hold persistently the fearless thought, the thought that you are afraid of nothing, that nothing can make you a coward.

If you are timid, if you suffer from shyness, just affirm that you will never again be afraid of anybody or anything, that you are going to hold your head up; assert your manhood or womanhood. Resolve that you will strengthen this weak link in your character.

Assuming an indifferent air often helps diffident, shy people. Just say to yourself:— "Other people are too busy to bother about me or to look at me and watch me, and, even if they do, it makes no difference to me. I am going to live in my own way."

If one is inclined to be retiring, shrinking, shy, the constant affirmation of the "I am" philosophy, the continual assertion, "I am a man made to do things, and I am going to do them,"— a little daily practise in cultivating courage and self-confidence, aggressiveness in pushing oneself into responsibility, will do wonders in building up, from a timid one, a bold, strong character.

If your parents and teachers tell you that you are dull and stupid, just deny it vigorously every time the suggestion comes to you. Constantly affirm that you are *not* stupid, that you have ability and that you are going to show the people who have disapproved of you that you can do what others do.

You will find that just in proportion as you increase your confidence in yourself by the affirmation of what you wish to be, your ability will increase.

No matter what other people may think about your ability never allow yourself to doubt that you can do or become what you long to do or become. Increase your self-confidence in every possible way, and you can do this to a remarkable degree by the power of self-suggestion.

There is a great asset, a splendid capital, in the personal suggestion. Always try to carry yourself in such a way and conduct yourself in such a manner as to suggest success, growth, improvement, superiority. The very reputation of growing, of being vigorously progressive, of being a man who does things, a man who carries weight and who stands for something in his community, is worth everything.

Every time you meet an acquaintance, whether conscious of it or not, you step upon the scales of his judgment, and he notes whether you weigh more or less than at the last meeting. Everybody you meet puts his measuring line about you and notes your girth.

If when they meet you people see that you

are looking upward, and that you are a little further on, a little higher up, that you are a little bigger man, stand for a little more than at the last meeting, you will establish yourself in their estimation as a coming man.

Never allow yourself to think meanly, narrowly, poorly of yourself. Never regard yourself as weak, inefficient, diseased, but as perfect, complete, whole. Never even think of the possibility of going through life a failure or a partial failure.

Failure and misery are not for the man who has seen the God-side of himself, who has been in touch with divinity. They are for those who have never discovered themselves and their God-like qualities.

Stoutly assert that there is a place for you in the world, and that you are going to fill it like a man. Train yourself to expect great things of yourself. Never admit even by your manner that you think you are destined to do little things all your life. If you practise and persistently hold the positive, producing, opulent thought, this mental attitude will some day make a place for you, and create that which you desire. Bear in mind that nothing will come to you without a sufficient cause, and that cause is mental.

Thoughts are forces, and by them we create ourselves and our conditions. These little force points are constantly chiseling, molding the character, fashioning the life. We can not get away from our thought. We must be like it.

Some one has said, "All human duty is boiled down into this, learn what to think and think it." St. Paul understood the philosophy of right thinking and he knew that these ideals held constantly in the mind will leaven the whole character and reshape the life. We are beginning to learn the profound philosophy in his advice: "Whatsoever things are true, whatsoever things are honest, whatsoever things are just, whatsoever things are pure, whatsoever things are lovely, whatsoever things are of good report; if there be any virtue, and if there be any praise, think on these things."

"*Think* on these things." He did not mean just to run them through the mind like water through a sieve, to merely pass them over lightly, but to *dwell* upon, contemplate them, hold them in the mind until they permeate the life, and become a permanent habit, a part of one's very being.

Just think of what the opposite advice would

mean, to dwell upon and harbor in the mind things foul, demoralizing, and debauching: impurity, hatred, revenge, discord, jealousy, and all the human passions to which St. Paul refers!

Dwelling upon the criminal thought produces the criminal. Dwelling upon the impurity suggestion makes the debauchee. St. Paul knew that it was the things that we *dwell* upon, *contemplate, think about habitually, concentrate the mind upon,* that determine the quality of the life. There never was better advice given by any human being than this of St. Paul's.

I can not get away from myself, no matter where I go. I am always environed by myself, horizoned by my mentality, encircled by my ideal, constantly influenced by my self-suggestion.

If my thought is narrow, I must live in a narrow world. If my thinking has been sordid, cold, and unsympathetic, I can not enjoy the broader and larger world others live in, for I have incapacitated myself to see it or to appreciate it. If I am mean, contemptible, and despicable in my conduct, then I am shut in by an ever-narrowing horizon, limited by the smallness and meanness of my thoughts.

If I am a person of mean, vicious habits, compelled to look through the bars behind which my vile or vicious thoughts and suggestions have imprisoned me, I can not complain of the loneness, the wretchedness of my condition. The cell which confines me is opened and shut by my will; locked by my volition.

Yet, while we can not get out of our atmosphere, we can change it by changing our thought, our attitude towards life. The quality of the thought determines the quality of the atmosphere. We have it in our power to live in a Paradise or a Hades. The thought determines it all.

It is now a well-established fact that victims of bad habits can be wonderfully benefited by resolving, upon retiring and dropping into unconsciousness, that they will have nothing more to do with drink, drugs, or the vicious habit which has been enslaving them.

How can you expect to get the maximum of efficiency when worry, fear, anxiety, discouragement, or melancholy are sapping twenty-five, fifty, or seventy-five per cent. of your mental energy? You must clear the mind of its enemies; otherwise you pay the penalty in exhausted vitality, in wasted energy.

The auto-jealous suggestion has shattered

numberless lives, even when there was no foundation whatever in fact. There is nothing short of crime that will create such a frightful havoc in the human mind as jealousy. What awful wrecks have been caused by this terrible fiend! Beautiful characters have been torn all to pieces and ruined in a few months by it. How many people have lived for years in perfect torture when there was absolutely no cause or real reason for it! What nameless crimes are committed by people who were kindly disposed, people naturally honest, but whose minds have been perverted, wrecked, by the harboring of this frightful enemy of peace and happiness!

The jealous man who thinks he has been seriously wronged, harbors the thought of revenge, and thinks of ways and means of getting "square" with his enemy until he finally takes his life. He may not have intended it at first, or even thought it possible; but his mind became abnormal by harboring the jealous thought. His desire for revenge grew until finally his mind was unbalanced and he committed the terrible deed.

Whatever weighs upon the mind, — the anxious thought, worry thought, fear thought, paralyzes its producing power.

It is marvelous what mental strength can be developed by the perpetual affirmation of vigorous fitness, strength, power, efficiency, — these are thoughts and ideals that make a strong man.

You can certainly use your brain power to better advantage than in dwelling upon and rehearsing unpleasant experiences. No matter if people do not use you right, just say to yourself: " I am too big to put myself upon the level of those who stoop to low-down, mean methods. Whatever other people do, I must act the part of a man. Life means too much to allow non-essentials to destroy my peace of mind or ruin my efficiency. I have to make good by delivering to the world in all its integrity the message which was given me at birth, which was marked out for me in my very constitution, and indicated in every fiber of my being. Because other people refuse to deliver their message or divert it, because they squander their time in that which impairs their ability and destroys their efficiency, is no reason why I should fail to deliver mine."

The next time you are in a discordant mood, when you feel cross and crabbed and out of sorts with everybody, when little things nettle you, and you can not get along with your office boy or stenographer, when you seem to antagonize those about you, when your brain is confused and you feel that you can not control yourself, just try this experiment: Stop work. Jump right up from your desk; leave whatever you are doing, and go out of doors. Walk a few blocks, or, if possible, slip out into the country and determine that you will drive out of your mind everything that fights against harmony and mental balance. Think of beautiful, harmonious things, pleasant things. Resolve that whatever comes you will be cheerful and poised, that you will not let little nagging things make a fool of you, that you will keep your mental instrument in tune.

In other words, resolve to be a man, to rise above the petty things of life. Just say to yourself, " What a ridiculous thing for a great, strong man, made to dominate the forces of the universe, to be completely upset, thrown off his base by trivial, foolish, insignificant things! " Resolve that you will go back to your work poised, self-possessed, self-respecting, and that you will put it through with power. Reason this way for a few minutes, in the open air if possible; take in full, deep breaths of fresh air, and you will return to your task a new man.

You will be surprised to find how well it will pay you to take time to put yourself in tune. No matter when you get out of tune, stop working, *refuse to do another thing until you are yourself,* until you are back on the throne of your mental kingdom.

The way to get the best out of yourself is to put things right up to yourself, handle yourself without gloves, and talk to yourself as you would to a son of yours of whom you expected great things.

When you go into an undertaking just say to yourself, " Now this thing is right up to me. I've got to make good, to show the man in me or the coward. There is no backing out."

Repeat to yourself some sterling, inspiring gritty bits of poetry or sayings such as, " Give me the man who faces what he must."

You will be surprised to see how quickly this sort of self-suggestion will brace you up and put new spirit in you.

I have a friend who has helped himself wonderfully by talking to himself about his conduct. When he feels that he is not doing all that he ought to, that he has made some foolish mistake or has failed to use good sense and good judgment in any transaction, when he feels that his stamina and his ambition are deteriorating, he goes off alone to the country, to the woods if possible, and has a good heart-to-heart-talk with himself something after this fashion:

"Now, young man, you need a good talking-to, a bracing-up all along the line. You are going stale, your standards are dropping, your ideals are getting dull, and the worst of it all is that when you do a poor job, or are careless about your dress and indifferent in your manner, you do not feel as troubled as you used to. You are not making good. This lethargy, this inertia, this indifference, if you're not very careful, will seriously cripple your career. You are letting a lot of good chances slip by you, because you are not as progressive and up-to-date as you ought to be.

"Your ideals need rubbing up. They are getting dim. In short, you are becoming lazy. You like to take things easy. Nobody ever yet amounted to much who let his energies flag, his standards drop, and his ambition ooze out. Now, I am going to keep right after you, young man, until you are doing yourself justice. This sort of take-it-easy policy will never land you at the goal you started for. You will have to watch yourself very closely, or you will be left behind.

" You are capable of doing something much better than what you are doing. You must start out to-day with a firm resolution to make the returns to-night from your work greater than ever before. You must be a conqueror, and make this a red-letter day. Bestir yourself, get the cobwebs out of your head, brush off the brain ash. Think, think, think, to some purpose! Do not mull and mope like this. You are only half-alive; get a move on you!"

This young man says he hauls himself " over the coals," as he calls it, every morning when he finds that his standards are down and he feels lazy and indifferent, in order to force himself up to a higher standard and put himself in tune for the day. It is the very first thing to which he attends.

He constantly chides himself for inaction, indifference, laziness, lack of energy. " Now, John," he says to himself, " Brace up. Make this day count. Don't let any opportunity slip. Seize it, wring every possibility out of it. Don't shrink from responsibility, no matter how hard or disagreeable, if there is valuable discipline in it, if it will help to make you more efficient, more self-confident. Don't try to get out of anything which will help you, which will make you a stronger and larger man."

He forces himself to do the most disagreeable tasks first, and does not allow himself to skip hard problems. " Now, don't be a coward," he says to himself, " If others have done this, you can do it."

By years of stern discipline of this kind he has done wonders with himself. He began as a poor boy living in the slums of New York with no one to take an interest in him, encourage, or push him. Though he had little opportunity for schooling when he was a small boy, he has given himself a splendid education, mainly since he was twenty-one. For many years he took up one study after another during his spare evenings, holidays, and odd moments, conquering and becoming proficient in each in its turn, until he has made himself a well-educated and broadly-read man. He excels as a conversationalist and is a most interesting character. I have never known any one else who carried on such a vigorous campaign in self-victory, self-development, self-training, self-culture as this young man has.

You habitual worriers, you people who have suffered the tortures of the damned for many years from disheartening experiences, the blue devils, suppose you call a halt and say to yourself, " Now, haven't I given about enough of the years of my life to worry and anxiety? For years I have been robbed of my sleep, have been made miserable a large part of my time by these detestable enemies of my comfort, my welfare, my prosperity, my health and my happiness.

" Now, John, isn't it about time you called a halt on all this miserable business? For a quarter of a century or more you have been a slave of worry, a miserable victim of anxiety. You have lived in constant terror of the expectancy of bad business, hard times, probable panics. There has never been a year since your young manhood that you have enjoyed the peace of mind, the satisfaction, and the contentment that is the birthright of every human being bearing the stamp of divinity."

To pull in the breath and blow it out again in constant fear and terror that something is going to happen is miserable existence, not living.

Every time you feel fear coming into your mind, shut it out as quickly as possible and apply the antidote — fearlessness, assurance. Picture yourself as absolutely fearless. Say to yourself, " I am no coward. Cowards fear and cringe and crawl but I am a *man*. Fear is a child's frailty. It is not for grown-ups. I positively refuse to stoop to such a degrading thing. Fear is an abnormal mental process and I am normal. Fear can not influence me, for I will not harbor it. I will not allow it to cripple my career."

There is no fate or destiny which puts one man down and another up. "It is not in our stars, but in ourselves, that we are underlings." He only is beaten who admits it. The man is inferior who admits that he is inferior, who voluntarily takes an inferior position because he thinks the best things were intended for somebody else. This is all nonsense. The world belongs to him who can conquer it. Good things belong to those who can take them by force of purpose and tenacity of determination. There is no power which parcels out good things to a favored few, and gives you and me inferior things.

The man who has acquired the power of keeping his mind filled with the thoughts which uplift and encourage, the optimistic thought, the cheerful, hopeful thought, has solved one of the great riddles of life.

VI. THE CRIME OF THE "BLUES"

VI. THE CRIME OF THE " BLUES "

Faith is the great antidote for worry. We fear because we can not see the way. Faith sees the way.

> " 'Tis easy enough to be pleasant
> When life flows on like a song,
> But the man worth while is the man
> With a smile when everything goes
> Dead wrong."

A troubled brain can not think clearly, vigorously, logically. Worry clogs the brain and paralyzes the thought.

> " Talk health. The dreary, never-ending tale
> Of mortal maladies is worn and stale;
> You can not charm or interest or please
> By harping on that minor chord, disease.

> " Talk happiness. The world is sad enough
> Without your woe."

THE man who can smile when things go wrong has a tremendous advantage over the person whose courage collapses just as soon as he is in a hard place. The man who can smile when everything seems to go against him shows that he is made of winning material, for no ordinary man can do this.

Carlyle says that some people are rich in the power to be miserable. Such people seem to have a genius for radiating mental poison. They project their gloom into your mind in spite of your efforts to protect yourself. They insist that they were born so, that they can not help having the "blues" and being despondent.

But this is all nonsense. No one was born to be miserable, to bring gloom into the world, or to make others unhappy. It was intended that we should all be joyously happy.

You have no more right to go about among your fellows with a vinegary expression on your face, radiating mental poison, spreading the germs of doubt, fear, discouragement, and despondency upon them, than you have to inflict bodily injuries. You have no more right to poison other people's happiness than their bodies.

It is a strange fact that many people are always at home to the "blues." Whenever a fit visits them, it seems to be welcome. They retail their miseries, go over and over their misfortunes, describe the symptoms of their suffering, their poverty, dwell upon all the hideous details, and tell everybody how cruel fate has been to them. They appear to have a morbid love for contemplating what has embittered their lives and hampered their progress. Thus they are always unconsciously etching these pictures of their thought enemies deeper and deeper into their character.

I know one of these victims of the "blues," a man who has such a genius for making other people miserable that it makes one blue to look at him. You would think by his expression that he were bearing on his shoulders all the troubles of mankind. It is difficult to smile or feel serene in his presence. No matter how enthusiastic or joyful you may be, his icy expression and discouraging conversation, his doubts and pessimism, chill you. Every time I go near him I feel as though I were running out of the sunshine into a dungeon.

The Creator placed us on this beautiful earth to be glad, not sad, not to go moping, whining, complaining, spreading pessimism, and peddling misery among our fellows.

"A cheerful, intelligent face," Emerson tells us, "is the end of culture." Every now and then we catch a glimpse of such a face, a face which has a light that was never on sea or land, which convinces us that the possessor has been in communion with something divine; a face so serene, calm, and cheerful that it makes us feel that we have had a glimpse into "the holy of holies." But how few such faces there are, compared with the number of sad, gloomy ones!

There is no place in civilization for the morose, gloomy, or despondent man. Nobody wants to live with him. Everybody is dejected and depressed in his presence, and tries to get away from him.

A melancholy, worrying mind encourages the development of disease by destroying the resisting power, and makes the body susceptible to it.

There is nothing more contagious than mental depression and the "blues."

How often we have seen a cheerful, optimistic, radiant soul enter a room where there was sadness, discouragement, despondency, and revolutionize every one present by the contagion of his irresistible humor, his laughter and fun-loving nature!

People who have periodical fits of the "blues" seem possessed by spirits of evil. It is impossible for them during such times to be civil, to say nothing of being courteous and kind, even to members of their family. They seem to think that when they are "blue" and discouraged they are excused from ordinary self-control, and they give vent to their feelings and make everybody miserable.

A great many people fail to reach a success which matches their ability because they are victims of their moods, which repel people and discourage business.

We avoid morose, gloomy people just as we avoid a picture which makes a disagreeable impression upon us. We instinctively turn to those who are beautiful, harmonious, sunny-souled.

People like and believe in us in proportion to our agreeableness and helpfulness. A morbid mind usually means a warped, twisted judgment.

Sometimes an entire household becomes infected by the presence of one sour, morose, discontented member. He is never satisfied with the weather, or with the plans of the rest of the family. He never wants to go out when or where the others do; when they want to drive in one direction, he is sure to want to go in some other one. In fact, his desires and plans are always opposed to theirs. He is out of harmony with his environment; he has no pleasure in common with any one about him. He is not only unhappy himself, but he prevents others from enjoying themselves.

That it is possible for these people to control their moods is often proved by some one unexpectedly calling upon the cross-as-a-bear person. A bad "spell" is sometimes instantly broken by the sound of a door-bell announcing company, and the victim is all smiles in a moment. It is like the habitual headaches which some women have, which are almost never known to occur on the day when they are to call upon the President or some other important personage. When necessary they can postpone their headaches for days. So "blue" people are ashamed to make bears of themselves and have tantrums when company is present.

I have in mind a man who suffers so terribly from "blue" fits that his whole appearance is completely changed while under their influence. He does not look like the same man. He is absolutely unfitted to attend to business, and even his best friends try to avoid him. His whole appearance is that of utter despair, of intense mental suffering.

Now, all this is a deplorable waste of splendid energy which might be used for something worth while.

Isn't it pathetic to see a strong, vigorous man, made to be a giant among the forces of the world, cowering, the abject slave of mental clouds which cast dark shadows over his life? Think of a man capable of leading hundreds or thousands of employees in a great enter-prise — a man of achievement, born to do great things — lying around for days, the vic-tim of the "blues," in the clutch of mental demons which he ought to be able to throttle in five minutes!

Everywhere we see people with great am-bitions doing most ordinary things, simply because there are so many days when they do not "feel like it" or when they are dis-couraged or "blue."

A man who is at the mercy of his disposition can never be a leader, a power among men. I know a brainy man who would be capable of very great things, but for the fact that he is a slave to his moods. You never know just how to approach him. If he is in a good humor he will be optimistic and in for everything that marks progress. But when he is "blue," or anything crosses him, all his standards are down; he is pessimistic, everything is going to the dogs. He will oppose his partner in every suggestion that involves expenditure; he wants to cut down expenses, cut off advertising, dis-charge help, — but the very next day, per-haps, if his mood has changed, he wants to pursue just the opposite course. So he see-saws, always way up or way down, — the victim of his moods, the slave of his treacher-ous disposition. If he gets a little discouraged, instead of resisting his mood and trying to overcome it, he succumbs to its influence and drops into the depths until his physical forces recuperate sufficently to throw off the bondage, become positive, creative, productive, and he becomes normal, hopeful, and cheerful again.

Discouragement colors the judgment. Peo-ple will do all sorts of foolish things under the pressure of fear. I have known men who own their own homes to sell property or do the most ridiculous things in order to raise money, because they were afraid they would come to grief in their business if they did not have it, when as a matter of fact there was no real cause for anxiety whatever. When you are at your wits' end and do not know which way to turn, you are in danger, for you are in no condition to plan anything or to do the best thing. You should do your planning when you are cool and calm.

You are not capable of correct judgment, of using good sense, when there is fear or doubt or despondency in your mind. Sound judg-ment comes from a perfectly working brain, unclouded, untroubled faculties. Never act upon that which is suggested when you are in a state of *fear* and *anxiety.* Carry out your plans, the course laid down when your brain was clear, your head level. When fear is in the mind the mental forces are scattered and we are not capable of vigorous concentration. Calmness, poise, balance, mental serenity are absolutely essential to the most effective thinking.

One reason why so many men do not get on in the world is because they decide important matters when the mind is in no condition to decide anything, when they are full of fear that they are going to have trouble, that they are going to sustain great loss, that there is going to be a financial panic. Things done under such pressure are never done wisely. Wisdom is what we want in an emergency, and wisdom only comes from a level head, a calm, clear brain.

There are men who are usually quite level-headed but who do the most foolish things when discouraged or suffering from the "blues," acting under the influence of their moods, when the brain is clouded, inexact, uncertain in its processes, instead of clear, active, and well balanced.

When a person is in trouble or an emergency confronts him, that is the time he needs a cool head, a clear brain, a sound judgment. If in such a condition, the moment you find fear or worry taking possession of you, you must not decide anything of importance. But you should at once neutralize this condition, antidote it by switching on the counter thought or mood. Just think yourself into calmness, poise. Get possession of yourself, get your mental balance, then you will be in a position to do the level-headed, sensible thing; but never act in important matters with a troubled, worried, anxious mind.

It was not intended that man should be a slave to his passions, a victim of his moods, or that he should need to consult his feelings as to whether he can perform the duties of a man, or carry out his life program. He was fashioned to rule, to dominate, to be ever master of himself, of his environment.

It is perfectly possible for a well-trained mind completely to rout the worst case of the "blues" in a few minutes; but the trouble with most of us is that instead of flinging open the mental blinds and letting in the sun of cheerfulness, hope, and optimism, we keep them closed and try to eject the darkness by main force, when one glimmer of soul-sunshine would dissipate the blackness-skeletons, the blue devils and black devils, which thrive in the darkness.

The art of arts is to learn how to clear the mind of its enemies, — enemies of our comfort, happiness, and success. It is a great thing to learn to focus the mind upon the beautiful instead of the ugly, the true instead of the false, upon harmony instead of discord, life instead of death, health instead of disease, and is not always easy, but it is possible to everybody. It requires only a little skilful thinking, the forming of the right thought habits.

If you absolutely refuse to entertain these black devils which rob you of your happiness, if you shut them out and deny them admission when you once see that they only have the reality which you give them, they will cease coming to you.

The best way to keep out darkness is to keep the life filled with light; to keep out discord, keep it filled with harmony; to shut out error, keep the mind filled with truth; to shut out ugliness, contemplate beauty and loveliness; to get rid of all that is sour and unwholesome, contemplate all that is sweet and wholesome. Opposite thoughts can not occupy the mind at the same time. Why not form the habit of entertaining your thought friends instead of your thought enemies; harmony friends, truth friends, beauty friends, instead of their opposites, which scrawl their hideous images and autographs upon your mind?

We should early form the habit of erasing from the mind all disagreeable, unhealthy, death-dealing thoughts. We should start out every morning with a clean slate. We should blot out from our mental gallery all discordant pictures, and replace them with the harmonious, uplifting, life-giving ones.

Think of a man like Roosevelt, with the ability to influence the world's civilization, waiting round in the morning on his moods before he can tell whether or not he can do a man's work, waiting till he " feels like it "! Think of such a man consulting some whim, some indisposition, as to whether he can perform some great task upon which, perhaps, the welfare of a nation depends!

No matter whether you feel like it or not, just affirm that you *must* feel like it, that you *will* feel like it, that you *do* feel like it, that you are normal and that you are in a position to do your best. Say it deliberately, affirm it vigorously, and it will come true.

Every time you catch yourself worrying or fretting or being anxious, unnaturally straining and striving and resisting, just pause for a few moments and say to yourself, "This is not living the life of an intelligent, thinking being, not the life of a real man. It is just the bare existence of an ignorant man who has never tasted the joys of normal living, broad existence."

The coming man will not say to himself, " I shall wait and see how I feel in the morning before laying out my program. If I do not have an attack of the 'blues' or dyspepsia, if my liver is all right, if my body does not say 'no,' I will go to my office and carry out my program." There will be infinitely more certainty in such a life than at present. Man will not be a victim of his moods, a slave of his feelings, his food, or the weather.

The next time you are in trouble, or feel discouraged and think you are a failure, just try the experiment of affirming vigorously, persistently, that all that is real *must* be good, for God made all that is, and whatever doesn't seem to be good is not like its Creator, can not be real. Persist in this affirmation. You will be surprised to see how unfortunate suggestions and adverse conditions will melt away.

The next time you feel the " blues " or a fit of depression or despondency coming on, just get by yourself, — if possible, after taking a good bath and dressing yourself becomingly — and give yourself a good talking-to. Talk to yourself in the same dead-in-earnest way that you would to your own child or a dear friend who was deep in the mire of despondency, suffering tortures from melancholy. Drive out the black, hideous pictures which haunt your mind. Sweep away all depressing thoughts, suggestions, all the rubbish that is troubling you. Let go of everything that is unpleasant, all the mistakes, all the disagreeable past; just rise up in arms against the enemies of your peace and happiness, summon all the force you can muster and drive them out. Resolve that no matter what happens you are going to be happy, that you are going to enjoy yourself. Just say to yourself, " This is an abnormal condition. Harmony is the everlasting fact. Discord must be an unreality, an absence of harmony, the reality." After a little practise of this sort you will be able to clear your mental sky of all clouds and keep it clear; keep your mind free from your enemies.

Sometimes, when we have been terribly depressed and suffering from the "blues," something has happened to change the whole mental attitude instantly — perhaps the arrival of a dear old friend of our youth, an old classmate, or some one whose wit and funny stories have driven the "blue" devils all out of our mind; perhaps a change of scene in traveling, or some happy experience or unexpected success, which has wrought the same result. Whatever it may be, the "blues" are always driven out by the opposite suggestion to that from which we are suffering. In other words, it is the antidote to our depression which kills them. The holding of the opposite thought in the mind drives out, kills or neutralizes the discord.

When you feel the "blues" coming on, concentrate your mind vigorously upon the very opposite qualities, hold the ideals of cheerfulness, confidence, gratitude, good-will towards everybody, and you will be surprised to see how quickly the enemies which were dogging your steps and making your life miserable will disappear, just as the darkness does when the shutters are opened and the light rushes in. We do not drive out the darkness, but introduce its antidote, light, which instantly neutralizes it. When you are low-spirited and feel the "blues" getting a grip upon you, just stop whatever you are doing and make a business of driving these enemies out of your mind, neutralizing them, killing them, by their opposite suggestions. You know perfectly well that a cheerful, beautiful thought, no matter how difficult it may be for you to hold it when you are suffering, will soon bring you relief. Assume the cheerful, hopeful virtue, if you have it not, and it will soon be yours.

The next time you feel jaded, discouraged, completely played out and "blue" you will probably find, if you look for the reason, that your condition is largely due to exhausted vitality, either from overwork, overeating, or violating in some way the laws of digestion, or from irregular habits of some kind.

You should try to get into the most interesting social environment possible, or seek some innocent amusement that will make you laugh and cheer you up. Some people find this refreshment in their own home romping with the children; others at the theater, in pleasant conversation, or in burying themselves in a cheerful, inspiring book.

If you feel like it, take a good, long nap.

I have a business friend who finds a wonderful help, when he reaches home tired and weary, in taking a hot bath and putting on his evening clothes. This change seems to make a new man of him.

Somehow our tired feelings, our troubles, trials, worries, and anxieties seem to cling to the very clothing which we have worn during the day, and the mere changing of it seems to change the current of the mind also.

The country is also a wonderful refreshener and healer of our woes. An hour's walk abroad under the open heaven after an exhausting, perplexing, soul-harrowing day's work, will often completely change one's whole mental attitude.

Seek the method of changing your mental attitude which is best suited to you, and you will be surprised to find the poison of fatigue fully neutralized, the whole atmosphere of your discouraged thought changed, and you will soon feel like a new person.

No matter how discouraging things look around you, learn to dominate your environment, to rise above the depressing influences; turn your back on the darkness, face the light, and the shadows will fall behind you.

How long would it take a man to cure himself of melancholia by holding the melancholy, gloomy, discouraged thought? You can not cure a " fit of the blues " with more " blues," more discouragement.

Give yourself a good heart-to-heart talk, just as you would if trying to help your dearest friend who was suffering from deep depression and great discouragement. Appeal to your own better nature. Try to shame yourself out of your foolishness. Show yourself how silly it is for a man to yield to such weaknesses. Say to yourself, "What would ever have become of Napoleon or Grant if they had been the slaves of their moods? What would Lincoln have done in a similar situation? Would he have played the baby and given up and gone about with a long face and dejected countenance, as though he had lost his last friend, his last dollar? If I am such a ' weak sister,' such a nonentity, the sooner I find it out the better."

When you look at it squarely, it is a very foolish, almost criminal, thing to go about this beautiful world, crowded with things to delight and cheer us, with splendid opportunities, showing a sad, dejected face, as though life had been a disappointment instead of a priceless boon. Just say to yourself, " I am a man and I am going to do the work of a man.

It's right up to me and I am going to face the situation."

I know of a woman who was prone to fits of depression, of the "blues," who conquered them by forcing herself to sing bright, joyous songs, and to play lively, inspiring airs on the piano whenever she felt an "attack" coming on.

The expelling power of a contrary emotion has a wonderful effect upon the mind. The cure for bad moods is to summon good ones to take their places in the thought and thus force them out.

Although it may be difficult, it is not impossible to reverse the mood.

If you are a victim of your moods, push right into the swim of things, and take an active part, with a real interest in what is going on around you. Associate with people. Be glad and happy, and interest yourself in others. Keep your mind off yourself. Get away from yourself by entering with zest into the family plans, or the plans and pleasures of others about you.

Self-depreciation is one of the characteristics of those suffering from the "blues." Most of us do not encourage ourselves enough by optimistic thinking, by auto-suggestion.

Hold the thought that there is nothing too good for God's child; that if you are made in His image you must partake of His likeness, that it was intended you should live in harmony, prosperity; that abundance and plenty are your birthright; that joy and gladness should encompass you.

Do not let anybody or anything shake your faith that you can conquer all the enemies of your peace and happiness, and that you inherit an abundance of all that is good.

The "blues" are often caused by exhausted nerve cells, due to overstraining work, long-continued excitement, or over-stimulated nerves from dissipation. It is the clamoring of exhausted nerve cells for nourishment, rest, or recreation. Multitudes of people suffer from despondency, melancholy, as a result of a run-down condition physically, owing to their irregular, vicious habits and a lack of refreshing sleep.

When you are feeling "blue" or discouraged, get as complete a change of environment as possible. Whatever you do, do not brood over your troubles or dwell upon the things which happen to annoy you at the time. Think the pleasantest, happiest things possible. Hold the most charitable, loving thoughts towards others. Say the kindest, pleasantest things. Make a strenuous effort to radiate joy and gladness to everybody about you. You will soon begin to feel a wonderful uplift; the shadows which have darkened your mind will flee away, and the sun of joy will light up your whole being.

Form a habit of never allowing in your mind thoughts or suggestions which call up unpleasant subjects or bitter memories, and which have a bad influence on you.

Every one ought to make it a life-rule to wipe out from his memory everything which has been unpleasant, unfortunate. We ought to forget everything which has kept us back, which has made us suffer, which has been disagreeable, and never allow the hideous pictures of distressing conditions to enter our minds again. There is only one thing to do with a disagreeable, harmful experience, and that is to bury it — *forget it.*

Dwelling on unfortunate experiences, mistakes only makes them bigger, blacker, more hideous. Forget them, thrust them out of your mind as you would a thief from your home. Say to them, "You have no power over me. You can not destroy my peace. You are not the truth of my being. The reality of me is divine. You can not touch principle, my real self. Only the good and the true are scientific realities, are absolutely real, all else, however real it may seem, is false, because there is only one Infinite Power in the universe. A supreme, perfect Being could not have made imperfection or discouragement. However real they seem, they are not realities, they are only the absence of harmony, the absence of truth."

We have all had the experience of suffering from things which eventually proved to be absolutely nothing but pure bogies of the imagination. A sensitive, imaginative mind can conjure up all sorts of hideous pictures, satanic images which torture as though they were real things.

Many people drive away the "blues" by reading something humorous, encouraging, or inspirational. I know some who get great help in reading the Psalms and Proverbs and the Saviour's sayings. There is a wonderful uplift, a healing balm in these inspired writings.

A physician, who is a nerve specialist, claims to have found a new remedy for the "blues." He advises his patients to try to smile under all circumstances, to compel themselves to laugh whether they feel like it or not. "Smile," he tells them. "Keep on smiling; do not stop smiling; just try *turning up the corners of your mouth*. See how it makes you feel, regardless of your mood." He has his patients remain in his office and smile, if only mechanically at first, and always urges them at least to keep an upward curvature of the corners of the mouth.

We were endowed with every faculty possible to enable us to enjoy life. Not stintedly, but in all its fulness, glory, completeness.

Unhappiness is as abnormal to our natures as disease. The spectacle which we see everywhere of anxious, wrinkled, unhappy faces, of gloomy, dissatisfied expressions, was never intended to mar this beautiful, glad earth. It is antagonistic to all nature. The pitiable thing about it all is that these enemies which rob us of our happiness, which dog our steps through life, are not realities at all, but merely an absence of harmony.

Don't estimate your future by the little troubles that confront you now. The black clouds which shut out your sun to-day will be gone to-morrow. Learn to look at life at long range and to put the right values upon things.

There are many times in the life of the youth who does things that are worth while, when he gets terribly discouraged, and thinks it easier to go back than to push on. But *there is no victory in retreating,* and we should never leave any bridges unburned behind us, or leave a way open for retreat to tempt our weakness, indecision, or discouragement. We should have courage and pluck and grit enough to push on, to keep going when things look dark and when seemingly insurmountable obstacles confront us.

Most people are their own worst enemies. We are all the time " queering " our life game by our vicious, tearing-down thoughts and unfortunate moods. Everything depends upon our courage, our faith in ourselves, in our holding a hopeful, optimistic outlook; and yet, whenever things go wrong with us, whenever we have a discouraging day or an unfortunate experience, a loss or any misfortune, we let the tearing-down thought, doubt, fear, discouragement, like a bull in a china shop, tear through our mentalities, breaking up and destroying the work perhaps of years of building-up, and we have to start all over again. Most of us work like the frog in the well. We climb up, only to fall back, and so lose all we gain.

When shall we learn that the wasteful, destructive thoughts are our great enemies? It takes but a few minutes to burn a house which it may have taken years to erect. A single stroke of the artist's brush will ruin a picture on which he may have been working for years. It is possible for the mind, through anger, jealousy, through pessimistic, melancholy, worrying, destructive thoughts, to spoil life's great picture which we have been many years in painting.

Try this experiment, the very next time you get discouraged or think you are a failure, that your work does not amount to much — turn about face. Resolve that you will go no further in that direction. Stop and face the other way, and *go* the other way. Every time you think you are a failure, it helps you to become one, for your thought is your life pattern. You can not get away from your thought. You can not get away from your ideals, the standard which you hold for yourself, and if you acknowledge in your thought that you are a failure, that you can't do anything worth while, as other people do, that luck is against you, that you don't have the same opportunity that other people have — your convictions will control the result.

When you turn round, your outlook will turn, and also your life.

The world has little use for the man who has not sand enough in him to brace up and be a man when he meets with failure.

There are thousands of people who have lost everything they valued in the world, all the material results of their lives' endeavor, and yet, because they possess a stout heart, an unconquerable spirit, a determination to push ahead which knows no retreat, they are just as far from real failure as before their loss; and with such wealth they can never be poor.

VII. CHANGE THE THOUGHT, CHANGE THE MAN

VII. CHANGE THE THOUGHT, CHANGE THE MAN

"Every art is but the result of some trained faculty of man."

The majority of people who make a failure in life do so because they never learn to guard and strengthen their weak points.

To correct deficiencies, remedy defective faculties, overcome peculiarities, and bring the mind into symmetry and poise so that it will express its maximum of power, will form a large part of the education of the future.

EARS ago, Central Park and other parts of upper New York City were made very unsightly by "squatters," people who camped on vacant lands and built all kinds of unbeautiful shanties on them. They made a great deal of trouble for the real owners of the land, especially those who resided abroad, because, after a protracted occupation, they would often dispute the ownership.

Many people are troubled with mental squatters, such as prejudice, bigotry, superstition, cowardice, jealousy, and all kinds of little peculiarities, which seem harmless at first but which gradually become so entrenched in their lives that it is very difficult to dispossess them.

One of the hardest lessons we have to learn is that we build our bodies by our thoughts; that they are discordant or harmonious, diseased or healthy, in accordance with our habitual thought and the thought of those who preceded us. There are those who, having learned this lesson, have had their countenances so altered in a single year by persistent right-thinking that one would scarcely recognize them. They have changed faces that were lined with doubt, disfigured with fear and anxiety, and scarred by worry or vice, to reflectors of hope, cheer, and joy.

Saint Paul showed scientific knowledge when he said: "Be ye transformed by the renewing of your mind;" that is, the changing, ennobling, purifying, refreshing of our thoughts.

Growth everywhere neutralizes decay. So long as we keep growing, *renewing* the mind, constantly reaching out for the new and progressive, the retrograding, disintegrating, aging, deteriorating processes can not be operative.

There is a law of perpetual renewal, a recreation constantly going on in us which is only interfered with by our adverse thought and discordant mental attitude.

The majority of us have had startling experiences of sudden mind renewal which have come unexpectedly and which have driven away the clouds from our minds, let in the sunshine of joy and happiness, and changed, at least for the time, our whole outlook upon life. When we have been discouraged and everything looked dark, some good fortune has perhaps come to us suddenly, or some jovial, congenial friend whom we have not seen for a long time has called upon us, or we have taken a trip into the country, and all our mental hurts have been healed by the new balm of suggestion. Sometimes, perhaps, when traveling we have come across a bit of entrancing scenery or some beautiful work of art about which we have read and have long wanted to see, and this stronger affection and interest — the marvelous suggestion of beauty, grandeur, and sublimity — has temporarily completely antidoted the worry thoughts or fear thoughts which a little while before were destroying our happiness.

Many people have an idea that the brain is not susceptible of any very great change; that its limits are fixed by the destiny of heredity, and that about all we can do is to give it a little polish and culture.

There are plenty of examples, however, of individuals who have completely revolutionized portions of their brains, and have made strong faculties of those which were weak at birth or deficient from lack of exercise. There are many instances where certain mental faculties have been almost entirely wanting, and yet have been built up so that they have powerfully buttressed the whole character.

Take courage, for instance. Many very successful people were once so completely devoid of this quality that the lack threatened to wreck their whole future. But through the help of intelligent training by parents and teachers they developed it until it became strong.

This was done by the cultivation of self-confidence, by holding the constant suggestion of courage in the young mind, by the contemplation of brave and heroic deeds, the reading of the life stories and works of great heroes, by the suggestion that fear is a negative quality — the mere absence of the natural quality of courage which is every man's birthright — and by the constant effort to do courageous deeds.

When the world was young the brain of man was very primitive, because the demand upon it was largely for self-protection and the acquisition of food, which called only for the development of its lower, its animal part. Gradually, however, there was a higher call upon it and a more varied development, until to-day, in the highest civilization, it has become exceedingly complex.

Every new demand of civilization makes a new call upon the brain, and, just as the physique of animals and men has been modified to meet varying conditions of climate and of maintenance, it develops faculties and powers to meet these fresh calls of a more complicated life.

The brain changes to meet these new demands upon it, develops new cells and strengthens weak ones, whenever the latter are brought into helpful activity.

Prof. Elmer Gates trained young dogs to develop some one sense, such as that of sight or sound. Other puppies of the same age and of the same litter would be kept in such a way that those particular brain cells would not be brought into activity, in which case they did not develop.

The parts of the brain presiding over color,

for example, were so trained that puppies could distinguish six or seven different shades of green and red.

The brain is modified by its condition of activity, the motives which actuate it, and the conditions which the individual has to meet. The brain of the man who leads a strenuous life in a great city is very different from that evolved by a quiet life on a farm. The great multiplicity of suggestions constantly held in the mind in city life tend to a more diverse development of brain power. The city man thinks quicker, his movements are quicker, his perceptions sharper because of the complexity and urgency of the demands upon him, so that he is really a different sort of man.

The brain is very adaptable. Each vocation makes a different call upon it and develops faculties and qualities peculiar to itself, so that as the various professions, trades, and specialties multiply, the brain takes on new adaptive qualities, thus giving greater variety and strength to civilization as a mass.

The clergyman, for instance, whose mind for years is centered upon spiritual things, develops very different brain characteristics from the lawyer, the merchant, or the architect.

It is easy to distinguish between a man whose life has been devoted to intellectual pursuits and one whose life has been spent in dealing in merchandise. Distinct faculties are developed and strengthened in the trader, such as sagacity, foresight, shrewdness, and the ability to systematize. Leadership calls out and often enormously develops certain faculties, such as initiative, the ability to use and control others, knowledge of human nature, and penetration.

An ambition-arousing environment is a powerful influence in modifying brain development, and the cultivation of ambition itself is a good illustration of the power of suggestion. A boy born and reared in a sparsely settled portion of the country may have great natural ability in a particular line, but, not coming in contact with the right stimulus to arouse his individual ambition, may never develop the power to do the greatest thing possible to him. On the other hand, if he should go to the city and get into an ambition-arousing atmosphere, his whole brain structure might be very materially changed.

How often we see examples of this sudden change in college men, especially those who have come from the country! The attrition of brain with brain, the contagion of ambition, and the coming in contact with ambition-arousing personalities often give the youth a glimpse of power which he never before realized he possessed, and thus alter his whole career.

There are many instances of stunted talents being quickly brought into vigorous activity by a change of occupation and conditions when the persons had no previous conception that they had any special ability in these lines.

We are just beginning to learn something of brain development possibilities; to discover something of the secret of brain-changing and of character-building which will some time revolutionize our methods of education.

Teachers and parents in the future will be trained in brain study. The coming teacher will know how to develop and strengthen deficient faculties by systematic brain-cell building; in enlarging brain cells which preside over certain faculties.

The late Professor James of Harvard said that the slightest thought changes the brain structure leaving its telltale work. The character of the thought is constantly changing the structure of the brain. The thought, whether good or bad, leaves its furrows in the brain substance. Every repeated thought tends to confirm a habit and makes the probability of any material change or reversal of the tendency so much the less. For example, there is nothing which will change a lovely character to one that is hideous, a sweet to a sour one, so quickly as the habit of holding revengeful, hateful thoughts. If you want to develop a lovable disposition, you know before you begin that you can not do it by holding hateful, jealous, envious, uncharitable thoughts.

Hold any particular thought in the mind persistently until it has formed grooves in the brain-tissue and become dominant in the brain structure, and you have permanently changed the character in that direction. You have only to change your mind to a desired direction, holding it there tenaciously until you have formed a new mental habit. Then you are, in that particular, a new creature.

A great many people who are conscious that they have considerable ability in most respects have a feeling of being very deficient or lacking in some one or more qualities, and this consciousness is a constant stumbling-block because it destroys that superb self-faith which is imperative for all great achievements.

These deficiencies or weaknesses are often due to lack of development by exercise of the portion of the brain where the qualities are located. It is perfectly possible and very practical gradually to build up and strengthen these deficient qualities or faculties, and to make them normal.

If you are deficient, if you have any weak faculties, traits, which you wish to strengthen, concentrate your thought upon the quality you desire. The cells presiding over that portion of the brain will be strengthened by holding your thought there. Holding a creative, affirmative, confident thought will strengthen the faculty, just as doubt and lack of confidence will weaken it.

If you are vacillating, if you lack decision, just assume a decisive mental attitude. Constantly affirm that you are able to decide wisely, firmly, finally. Do not allow yourself to think that you are weak.

Sometimes quite strong faculties remain practically undeveloped because our previous occupation or mental activities have not called them into play, and they have been lying dormant.

The science of brain-building will teach us how to prevent and how to eliminate idiosyncrasies and peculiarities and how to strengthen weaknesses which now handicap so many of us. We shall learn that *symmetrical* brain development is what gives power, and that to develop some particular faculty or faculties — and allow others, which are perhaps equally as important, to atrophy and shrivel from disuse — is not scientific education, and that this one-sided development is a curse to our civilization and a menace to sanity.

If you wish to cultivate or to improve a weak or deficient faculty, just hold the picture of it in its perfect form. Do not hold the defective, faulty image. Think of it and live it in your thoughts as you would like to have it, and try in every way to exercise it so that new and better brain cells will be formed and the weak ones strengthened.

Not only can we strengthen mental weaknesses and deficiencies, but it is perfectly possible to increase the general ability through the power of suggestion. Indeed, the susceptibility of all the mental faculties to improvement, to enlargement, is something remarkable.

Sometimes very strong faculties are latent until especially aroused. There are many people who pass for cowards; who are humiliated because they apparently have so little courage, when, if they only knew how, they could strengthen this deficient faculty wonderfully by holding the courageous ideal; by thinking

and doing the courageous deed; by carrying
the thought of fearlessness; by reading about
heroic lives; by constantly thinking the heroic
thought and trying to live it. Courage may
be small in a person because it has never been
called into sufficient exercise. It may need
only to be aroused. There are many people
living lives of mediocrity who might do great
things, might become mental giants if their
dormant faculties were aroused, their general
ability improved and enlarged.

Learn to assert stoutly the possession of
whatever you lack. If it is courage or staying
power, assert these qualities as yours by divine
right. Bear in mind that they are your birth-
rights and stoutly refuse to give them up. Be
thoroughly convinced that they belong to you,
that you actually possess them, and you will
win.

We tend to become like our aspirations. If
we constantly aspire and strive for something
better and higher and nobler, we can not help
improving. The ambition that is dominant in
the mind tends to work itself out in the life.
If this ambition is sordid and low and animal,
we shall develop these qualities, for our lives
follow our ideals.

Many people have the impression that their

ability is something that is inherited, and that while they may polish it a little, they can not add to it or enlarge it. But we are beginning to see that all the mental faculties are capable of very great enlargement. The brain power can be increased immensely by systematic thought education. In fact, there is not a single faculty which can not be very materially improved in a comparatively short time.

The time will come when one of the principal objects of education will be the poising of the mind; balancing it, making it symmetrical, and strengthening its weak cells by the building up of defective or deficient faculties, by scientifically exercising that portion of the brain which presides over them.

We shall ultimately learn that vicious and criminal tendencies, even when hereditary, may be educated out of the brain, and symmetry and power be obtained.

There is every evidence in the human plan that man was made to express completeness, wholeness — not a half nor a fraction of himself; a hundred, not twenty-five nor fifty per cent. of his possibilities; made to express excellence, not mediocrity, and that the half lives and quarter lives which we see everywhere are abnormal.

The shrewdest thing a man can do is to put himself beyond the possible self-wreckage from his own deficiencies and weaknesses and vicious tendencies.

Instead of trying to root out a defect or a vicious quality directly, cultivate the opposite quality. Persist in this, and the other will gradually die. *"Kill the negative by cultivating the positive."*

The craving for something higher and better is the best possible antidote or remedy for the lower tendencies which one wishes to get rid of.

When the general habit of always aspiring, moving upwards and climbing to something higher and better is formed, the undesirable qualities and the vicious habits will fade away; they will die from lack of nourishment. Only those things grow in our nature which are fed. The quickest way to kill them is to cut off their nourishment.

The impression held by parents and educators for centuries that mental qualities, traits and faculties are not cultivatable or subject to change to any great extent has been entirely exploded. In the little kindergarten plays designed to develop the different faculties, it is found that in the courage plays, for example, the timid, shrinking, bashful children gradually develop greater confidence, and, as they become experts in their parts, their shyness, self-consciousness, and fear entirely disappear.

The little joy plays, laughter plays, or cheerful plays have a marked influence upon children, especially when they have very little fun in their home life and are inclined to sadness and melancholy. Their whole expression changes very quickly in response to suggestion in such plays.

One of the cruelest things one can do to another is to reproach him for his deficiencies, peculiarities, or weaknesses. What such a person wants is encouragement and help, not additional handicap.

If a girl is less favored by facial beauty than her companions, instead of being constantly reminded of it she should be taught to hold the beauty ideal until it modifies her features. She should be told that soul beauty infinitely transcends physical beauty; that, by constant self-improvement and trying to help others, she can make herself so fascinating in manner, so unselfishly interesting, that no one would notice any physical lack or irregularity of feature or form.

Multitudes of people keep their minds so

trammeled by ignorance and superstition, so deformed by worry, crippled by fear and anxiety, that their brains can not express a tenth of their maximum creative power. They never know what complete liberty means. Their minds are restricted by terrors, by hatreds, by unrestrained passions which make effective thinking impossible. But it is not so very difficult to remedy these things if we understand the law of habit formation. The whole thing is simply a question of unraveling the ball in the opposite direction from which it was wound.

Take, for instance, the hot-tempered habit. Self-control is not so very difficult if you just cut off the fuel which feeds the fire; but when the hot blood rushes through your brain you feed the conflagration with the suggestion of angry words and an angry physical attitude, and if you continually raise your voice, thresh your arms, throw things across the room, and proceed to break things up generally, you can work yourself up into a terrific rage in a very few moments.

If, on the other hand, you cut off the fuel which feeds the burning passion and apply the antidote — just as you would put out a fire with water — and, if only mechanically, try to apply the love-thought, the kindly, good-will thought, the charitable thought, the do-as-you-would-be-done-by philosophy, you will be surprised to see how quickly these antidotes will put out the fire. You will then have, instead of a destructive conflagration raging through you, burning up your energy and consuming your vitality, a kindly good-will glow gradually stealing over your entire being, and in a very few moments you will be at peace with all the world.

The mother calls out of the child the ideal qualities which she sees in it. Many mothers make the mistake of forever looking for the bad in the child, trying to correct the evil, up-root and drive it out. This is like trying to eject the darkness from a room without opening the shutters and letting in the light. "I can not sweep the darkness out, but I can shine it out," said John Newton.

Parents, teachers, reformers are beginning to see that they call out of those whom they wish to help just what they see in them, because their suggestive thought arouses its affinities. The subject *feels* their thought. If it is a helpful, inspiring one, it tends to uplift him. If, on the other hand, it is concentrated upon his defects, these very qualities which they try to erase are only etched deeper and made more indelible.

The same principle applies to our own imperfections; our own unfolding. If we over-emphasize the bad in ourselves, if we are always criticizing our shortcomings and weaknesses and castigating ourselves for not doing better, we only deepen the unfortunate pictures in our consciousness and make them more influential in our lives.

On the other hand, if we visualize the larger possible man or woman and see only what is sublime in ourselves, we shall be able to make infinitely more of ourselves and open up the glorious possibilities of what may properly be called a divine development.

What a great thing it would be if we could learn always to think of ourselves, or of others when we are talking with or about them, as the image and likeness of perfection, instead of as the weak, the debauched image, the mere burlesque of the man God made!

One reason why some clergymen have been able to revolutionize so many lives is because they looked to the God-side of people, and hence, no matter how low they had fallen, saw hope for them. However blurred it seemed, they could see the God-image beneath.

No one can help another very much when he sees in him a hopeless picture. On the other hand, you can make a person do almost anything when you show him his possibilities and make him believe in himself.

The great secret of Phillips Brooks's marvelous influence upon people who had lost their self-respect and were wallowing in beastly habits was that he reflected back to them the lost image of their possible divine selves. This picture gave them hope and encouragement, for, as he said, no man will ever be willing to live a half life when he has once seen that it is a half life.

The world has made marvelous strides along material lines in multiplying efficiency of machinery; increasing facilities for rapid transportation and quick communication of thought; in our educational system, in the way of learning things; in inventions, in our methods of doing business and in controlling the forces of nature; but we have not made very great progress in the art of increasing human efficiency in scientific mind-building, mind-changing, mind-construction, man-building.

The future physician will be a trained psychologist, a real educator of the people, showing them how to think properly; explaining how right thought makes right life; that their bodily conditions are simply reflections and outpicturings of their mental attitudes, present and past, and how, by changing the thought they can change the life.

If invalids and people in poor health could only hold persistently the perfect image of themselves, and, no matter how much it might howl in pain for recognition, refuse to see the sick, discordant, imperfect image, the harmony thought, the truth thought would soon neutralize their opposites and they would be well.

All reforms and all mental healing must result from changing the mind; from a complete reversal of the mental attitude; a turning about and facing the other way.

In proportion as the healer is able to annihilate the sick image, the disease image, and picture vividly the God-man, the divine image in all its wholeness and completeness, he is successful. When the mind is changed the man is changed.

VIII.   THE PARALYSIS OF FEAR

VIII. THE PARALYSIS OF FEAR

Fear and worry make us attract the very things we dread.

The fear habit impairs health, shortens life and paralyzes efficiency.

Doubt and fear mean failure; faith is an optimist, fear a pessimist.

Fear in all its different phases of expression, such as worry, anxiety, anger, jealousy, timidity, is the greatest enemy of the human race. It has robbed man of more happiness and efficiency, has made more men cowards, more people failures or forced them into mediocrity, than anything else.

HE effect which Halley's Comet recently had upon the ignorant and superstitious people in all parts of the world was something appalling. Multitudes were completely prostrated and thousands made ill with terror; many became violently insane and scores committed suicide. A great many peasants in European countries were in momentary expectation that the comet would annihilate the earth, and in some towns messengers went through the streets

blowing horns to awaken the people to the fact that the world was coming to an end.

The expectation that the earth would be burned up by the comet forced men to confess murder and other crimes of which they were not even suspected. Mothers poisoned their children. People ordered their coffins from undertakers in order to be ready for the terrible calamity. Several persons actually dropped dead at the first sight of the comet.

In the poorer sections of New York and other large cities great processions of people repeating their prayers paraded the streets with crucifixes in their hands, their terror-stricken faces turned toward the sky. Many were seen on their knees praying in the streets.

There was great excitement among the negroes in the South, where all-night services were held in the churches, numbers professing salvation in an effort to prepare themselves for the fatal day when the earth would be destroyed by the comet's tail. In numerous places the farms and fields were practically denuded of help, the hands positively refusing to work.

In Pennsylvania thousands of miners refused to go to their posts, while operations were entirely suspended in several mines.

Similar instances could be multiplied by the thousands.

The comet gave an unusual opportunity for quacks to trade upon the superstitious fears of the ignorant. The officers of one of the ocean liners reported that a thriving business was being conducted in some of the West Indian Islands by selling " anti-comet " pills at a dollar a box. As these were very bitter they were supposed to be especially efficacious.

All this would not seem so strange in the Dark Ages when people were densely ignorant, but it certainly is lamentable in these progressive days that any large number of people, with all of the advantages of education and unlimited opportunities for enlightenment, should be so ignorant as to fear harm from a comet which has been visiting the earth periodically and harmlessly for untold centuries.

Despite all our boasts of education, environment, and freedom, and of the advantages which have come to us through many centuries of experience, vast multitudes of people are still victims of numberless silly superstitions and fears that enslaved their barbaric ancestors.

Tens of thousands of women in this country believe, for instance, that if two people look in a mirror at the same time, or if one thanks another for a pin, or if one gives a knife or any sharp instrument to a friend, it will break up friendship. They believe that if a young lady is presented with a thimble she will be an old maid; that when leaving a house it is unlucky to go back after any article which has been forgotten, and, if one is obliged to do so, one must sit down in a chair before going out again; that if a broom touches a person while some one is sweeping, bad luck will follow; that it is unlucky to change one's place at table, etc.

I know the wife of an editor of a prominent magazine who was completely upset by finding peacock decorations in a room where she was visiting. She predicted all sorts of ill luck for the occupants.

Think of a college graduate baseball manager refusing to go on with a game, when thousands of spectators were waiting, until two bats which were crossed were separated, in order to prevent a hoodooed game!

Years ago, a man took an opal to a New York jeweler and asked him to buy it. He said that it had brought him nothing but bad luck, that since it had come into his possession he had failed in business, there had been much sickness in his family, and all sorts of misfortunes had befallen him. He refused to keep the cursed thing any longer. The jeweler examined the stone and found it was not an opal after all, but *an imitation.*

In some communities it is considered a crime to rock an empty cradle, because it betokens that the cradle will always be empty, by reason of the death of the babies born to the owner.

Think of intelligent American women being made ill because they are obliged to remove their wedding ring, believing that " until death do us part " refers to the ring as well as to the couple, and that the severing of the ring from the finger betokens the severing of the husband and wife!

Multitudes of intelligent people are afraid to start on a journey or to undertake anything of importance upon Friday, — as though a mere arbitrary name of the sixth day of the week, adopted for man's convenience should possess intelligence, force, or life!

Some time ago a bank failed in San Francisco because its president had followed the counsel of a medium as to his investments. He was foolish enough to believe in the advice of a dead financier with whom the medium assured him she had communicated rather than in common-sense and his own experienced judgment.

The dire predictions of quack fortune-tellers are responsible for infinite misery and a great many deaths. Scores of people have committed suicide under their influence.

It is incredible that intelligent people should be so mentally warped and unbalanced by astrologers, palmists, mediums, and fortune-tellers that many of them order their entire lives by their advice. Of course, many of the things which the fakers predict do happen, especially when the whole mental attitude of the gullible victim is turned toward the prediction and all his faith centered in it to bring it about. Mental concentration, faith and conviction, as a matter of fact, are what make things happen everywhere.

The minds of children often get an unfortunate twist, which later in life proves fatal, from having their fortunes told at some fair or place of amusement, or from the superstitious ideas impressed upon them from infancy by ignorant mothers or nurses.

It is a terrible thing to fill a child's susceptible mind with senseless superstitions, because many people never outgrow their influence, and their whole lives are shadowed by them.

What a curious contradiction of human nature it is which causes people to put so much emphasis upon the great power of destiny or fate, but makes them believe they can circumvent or get around it by resorting to such silly devices as carrying rabbits' feet, wishbones, or horse-chestnuts in their pockets! Think of intelligent people bearing the stamp of divinity doing such insane things as spitting on the right shoe before putting it on, picking up every hairpin and hanging it upon the first rusty nail they see; picking up every pin that is pointed toward them, in order to ward off misfortunes!

We often hear intellectual people say that superstitions are harmless; but nothing is harmless which makes a man believe that he is a puppet at the mercy of signs and symbols, omens and inanimate relics, that there is a power in the world outside of Omnipotent Intelligence working in opposition, trying to do harm to mortals.

While many great men have had superstitions, they would have been much greater without them, for superstition tends to weaken the mind. Anything which makes us believe in or depend upon any force or power outside of the Omnipotent Creative Power, of which we are a part, or to believe that there is a force that can circumvent or interfere with the regular order and law which govern the universe, lessens our self-confidence, self-respect, and power by so much.

Common-sense people may smile at you when you parade your superstitions, but they will think less of you while they are doing it, because their confidence in your good sense, your level-headedness and ability will be shaken.

Everywhere we see people doing little mediocre things who are capable of doing much better, and would do them but for the fact that they are held back, tied down, by the bonds of silly superstition.

If you are ambitious to make the most of your ability, cut the cords of superstition. Get rid of the chains which enslave you, which cripple your self-reliance. No one can do great things until he gets mental freedom from the slavery of fear and superstition.

Everywhere we see splendid ability tied up and compelled to do mediocre work because of the suppressing, discouraging influence of fear. On every hand there are competent men whose efforts are nullified and whose ability to achieve is practically ruined by the development of this monster, which will in time make the most decided man irresolute; the ablest man timid and inefficient.

Fear is a great robber of power. It paralyzes the thinking faculties, ruins spontaneity, enthusiasm, and self-confidence. It has a blighting effect upon all one's thoughts, moods, and efforts. It destroys ambition and efficiency.

Not long ago a publication interviewed twenty-five hundred persons and found that they had over seven thousand different fears, among them fear of loss of position, fear of approaching want, fear of contagion, fear of the development of some hidden disease or of some hereditary taint, fear of declining health, fear of death, fear of premature burial, and multitudes of superstitious fears.

There are plenty of people who are simply afraid to live, scared to death for fear they will die. They do not know how to dislodge the monster fear that terrifies them, and it dogs their steps from the cradle to the grave.

With thousands of people the dread of some impending evil is ever present. It haunts them even in their happiest moments. Their happiness is poisoned with it so that they never take much pleasure or comfort in anything. It is the ghost at the banquet, the skeleton in the closet. It is ingrained into their very lives and emphasized in their excessive timidity, their shrinking, self-conscious bearing.

Some people are afraid of nearly everything. They are afraid of a draught; afraid of getting chilled or taking cold; afraid to eat what they want; to venture in business matters for fear of losing their money; afraid of public opinion. They have a perfect horror of what Mrs. Grundy thinks. They are afraid hard times are coming; afraid of poverty; afraid of failure; afraid the crops are going to fail; afraid of lightning and tornadoes. Their whole lives are filled with fear, fear, fear.

There are many people who have a dread of certain diseases. They picture the horrible symptoms, the loss in personal attractiveness, or the awful pain and suffering that accompany the disease, and this constant suggestion affects the appetite, impairs nutrition, weakens the resisting power of the body, and tends to encourage and develop any possible hereditary taint or disease tendency.

It is well known that during an epidemic, even before any physical contact by which the contagion could have been imparted to them was possible, people have developed the disease they feared, simply because they allowed their minds to dwell on the terrible thing they dreaded.

In 1888 there was an epidemic of yellow fever at Jacksonville, Florida, and a very extensive epidemic of fear throughout the Southern States. The latter disease, a mental malady, was much more contagious than the former and much less amenable to treatment; it visited every little town, village, and hamlet in several States, and many victims died of it.

There are many cases in medical history of prisoners who were so terrified when they came in sight of the guillotine or the gallows, that they died before they were executed.

Many soldiers in battle who thought they were mortally wounded have died, when, as a matter of fact, they had not been touched by the bullets or shells and not even a drop of blood had been shed. Violent fear has been known to bleach the hair in a single night, and terror of some great impending doom or danger to take years out of a life.

A medical journal reports the case of a German physician who when riding over a bridge saw a boy struggling in the water and rushed to the rescue, and when he pulled the lad to shore, found it was his son. His friends did not know the man next day; his hair had turned completely white.

It is well known that when Ludwig of Bavaria learned of the innocence of his wife, whom he had caused to be put to death on suspicion of her unfaithfulness, his hair became as white as snow within a couple of days.

When Charles the First attempted to escape from Carisbrooke Castle, his hair turned white in a single night. The hair of Marie Antoinette was suddenly changed by her great distress. On a portrait of herself which she gave to a friend she wrote, " Whitened by affliction."

Authentic instances of the hair turning white in a few hours or a night through fear or sudden shock could be multiplied indefinitely.

This power of fear to modify the currents of the blood and all the secretions, to whiten the hair, paralyze the nervous system, and even to produce death, is well known. Whatever makes us happy, whatever excites enjoyable emotions, relaxes the capillaries and gives freedom to the circulation; whatever depresses and distresses us, disturbs or worries us, in fact, all phases of fear and anxiety, contract these blood vessels and impede the free circulation of the blood. We see this illustrated in the pale face caused by fear or terror.

Now, if terror can furnish such a shock to the nervous centers as to whiten the hair in a few hours, what shall we say of the influence of chronic fear poison, worry and anxiety poison acting upon the system for many years, thus causing a slow death instead of a quick one?

How suicidal chronic anxiety is! Few people realize that the system is kept continually poisoned by it. It is a strange thing that after all the centuries of experience and enlightenment the human race has not learned positively to refuse to be perpetually tortured by enemies of its happiness,—fear, anxiety, worry. It certainly would seem as though the race could have found some way out of this needless suffering long ago. But we are still frightened by the same ghosts: worry, anxiety; from the cradle to the grave we are the victims of these mental enemies, which we could easily destroy, neutralize, by simply changing the thought.

Who can estimate the fear and suffering caused by the suggestion of heredity? Children are constantly hearing descriptions of the terrible diseases that carried off their ancestors, and naturally watch for the symptoms in themselves.

Think of a child growing up with the constant suggestion thrust into his mind that he has probably inherited cancer or consumption, or something else which caused the death of one of his parents and will probably ultimately prove fatal to him! This perpetual expectancy of disease has a very depressing influence and handicaps the child's chances at the very beginning of his life.

Children who live in a fear atmosphere never unfold normally, but suffer from arrested development. Their stunted, starved bodies do not attain their normal growth; the blood-vessels are actually smaller, the circulation slower, and the heart weaker under the influence of fear.

Fear depresses, suppresses, strangles. If it be indulged in, it will change a positive, creative mental attitude into a non-productive, negative one, and this is fatal to achievement. The effect of fear, especially where the fear thought has become habitual, is to dry up the very source of life. Love that casteth out fear has just the opposite effect upon the body and brain. It enlarges, opens up the nature, gives abundant life-cells and increases the brain-power.

Fear works terrible havoc with the imagination, which pictures all sorts of dire things. Faith is its perfect antidote, for, while fear sees only the darkness and the shadows, faith sees the silver lining, the sun behind the cloud. Fear looks down, and expects the worst; faith looks up and anticipates the best. Fear is pessimistic, faith is optimistic. Fear always predicts failure, faith predicts success. There can be no fear of poverty or failure when the mind is dominated by faith. Doubt can not exist in its presence. It is above all adversity.

A powerful faith is a great life-prolonger, because it never frets; it sees beyond the temporary annoyance, the discord, the trouble, it sees the sun behind the cloud. It knows things will come out right, because it sees the goal which the eye can not see.

People of long lives have a strong faith; it may not quite agree with our own expression of faith religiously, but they have faith as a perpetual companion assuring them that things will come out right in the end.

Worry has disqualified many a man from paying his debts by sapping his energy, ruining and impairing his productive capacity.

Faith keeps a man from worrying and enables him to use his resourcefulness, inventiveness, to infinitely greater advantage.

The man who is paralyzed through fear is in no condition to make the best of what he has. If he is in a tight place, all of his faculties should be intact. If he worries, he only incapacitates himself from doing his best. The calm, balanced mind gives assurance, confidence.

No matter what your need is, put it into the hands of faith. Do not ask how or why or when. Just do your level best, and have faith, which is the great miracle worker of the ages.

Chronic worriers are always deficient in faith. The man who has a vigorous faith that a Power infinitely wiser than he is directing and guiding the affairs of the universe, and that everything is progressing towards the grand consummation of the omniscient, omnipotent Planner, that all discord of every kind will ultimately be swallowed up in harmony, that truth will finally triumph over all error, that everything in the universe, however it may seem to be contradicted, is tending towards the final consummation of a race-plan so superb, so beneficent, so magnificent, that no human mind could comprehend it, — such a man does not worry. When disappointments, losses, reverses, catastrophes, come to him, his mental balance is not disturbed, because his faith looks beyond misfortune and sees the sun behind the clouds, the victory beyond the seeming defeat. No matter what happens, he knows that " God is in His heaven and all's right with the world."

Many people fail by constantly stopping to wonder how they will finally come out, whether they will succeed or not. This constant questioning of the outcome of things creates doubt, which is fatal to achievement.

The secret of achievement is concentration. Worry or fear of any kind is fatal to mental concentration and kills creative ability. The mind of a Webster could not concentrate when filled with fear, worry, or anxiety. When the whole mental organism is vibrating with conflicting emotions, efficiency is impossible. The real suffering in life is not so great, after all. The things which make us prematurely old, which wrinkle our faces, take the elasticity out of our step, the bloom from the cheek, and which rob us of joy are not those which actually happen.

An actress renowed for her great beauty has said: " Anybody who wants to be good-looking must never worry. Worry means ruination, death and destruction to every vestige of beauty. It means loss of flesh, sallowness, tell-tale lines in the face and no end of disasters. Never mind what happens, an actress must not worry. Once she understands this, she has passed a milestone on the high road to keeping her looks."

What a good thing it would be if the habitual worrier could see a picture of himself as he would have been if his mind had always been free from worry! What a shock, but what a help it would be for him to place beside it another picture of himself as he actually is — prematurely old, his face furrowed with deep worry and anxiety wrinkles, shorn of hopefulness and freshness, a picture of a man appearing many years older than in the other, where he would seem vigorous, optimistic, hopeful, buoyant!

In nearly all forms of religion fear has played a great part. The priesthood in the Middle Ages found it most effective to draw the ignorant masses to the churches and to control their acts. Ignorance is so susceptible to fear that in all periods of the world's history the temptation to take advantage of it has been very great.

Who can estimate the terrible effects of the fear of a physical hell; of eternal punishment? This doctrine has for centuries cast a gloom over the human race.

The central idea in the origin of churches was to furnish a way of relief from fear in all its various forms of expression. In other words, it was an effort of human beings to furnish relief from the things which trouble and worry, from the heart-aches of mankind. And yet these very churches have unconsciously encouraged the development of fear by using it as a weapon to whip people into church attendance, the performance of church duties, etc.!

What a terrible thing it is for a human being, made in the Creator's image, to live in perpetual fear that something terrible is going to happen to him, here or hereafter; that he is a mere puppet of circumstance; that a cruel fate is likely at any time to appear in the guise of some dread disease or calamity!

How can one learn to develop the highest ideals of life while he holds in the mind the constant fear of death; the dread of possible momentary dissolution; the possibility of having all his life plans strangled, snuffed out in an instant? Nothing enduring, nothing per-

manent or solid can be built with these night-
mare fears in the mind. The doleful, perpetual preparation for imminent death is abnormal and fatal to all growth; fatal to
achievement; fatal to happiness.

What is fear? Whence comes its power to
strangle and render weak, poor, and inadequate
the lives of so many? It has absolutely no
reality. It is purely a mental picture, a bogy
of the imagination, and the moment we realize
this it ceases to have power over us. If we
were all properly trained and were large
enough to see that nothing outside of ourselves
can work us harm, we would have no fear of
anything.

I differ from a physican who has recently
stated that the emotion of fear is as normal to
the human mind as that of courage. Nothing
is normal which destroys one's ability, blights
self-confidence, or strangles ambition. This
physician evidently confuses the faculties of
caution, prudence, and forethought with the
fear thought which blights, destroys, and kills.
The former were given us for our protection, to keep us from doing things which
would be injurious, but there is not a saving
virtue in fear, in the sense in which the word
is ordinarily used. Its presence cripples the

normal functions of all of the mental faculties. The Creator never put into His own image that which would impair efficiency, cause distress, or destroy happiness. The exercise of every normal faculty or quality tends to enhance, promote, and strengthen the best in us, otherwise it would not be normal. We might as well say that discord is a good thing as to say that fear is normal.

As a nation we are too sober, too sad, and take life too seriously. Our theology and our creeds have too much anxiety and fear, too much sadness and seriousness and too little joy and gladness; too much of the shadow and too little of the sunshine of the soul in them; too much of the hereafter and too little of the now and here.

Fear benumbs initiative. It kills confidence and causes indecision, makes us waver, afraid to begin things, suspect and doubt. Fear is a great leak in power. There are plenty of people who waste more than half of their precious energy in useless worry and anxiety.

We can neutralize a fear thought by applying its natural antidote, the courage thought, the assuring, confident, faith thought, just as the chemist destroys the corrosive power of an acid by adding its opposite — an alkali.

Men can not get the highest quality of efficiency and express the best thing in them when their minds are troubled and when worry is sapping their vitality and wasting their energy. The worried, angry, troubled brain can not think vigorously or clearly.

Worry is but one phase of fear, and always thrives best in abnormal conditions. It can not get much of a hold on a man with a superb physique, a vigorous mentality, a man who lives a clean, sane life. It thrives on the weak — those of low vitality and exhausted energy, and especially on people who live vicious lives.

Worrying about disease produces disease.

The great *desideratum* is to keep one's physical, mental, and moral standards so high that the disease germ, the worry germ, the anxious germ, can not gain a footing in our brain. Our resisting power ought to be so great that it would be impossible for these enemies to get into the brain or body.

To keep ourselves perfectly free from our worry enemies, everything we do must be done sanely. No matter how honest we may be or how hard we may try to get on, if we are not sane in our eating, in our exercise, in our thinking, in our sleeping and living generally, we leave the door open to all sorts of trouble. There are a thousand enemies trying to gain entrance into our system and attack us at our vulnerable point.

It is the cool, calm, serene man, who when away from his work shows that he is a big enough man to leave business affairs to business hours; shows that he does not need to go home and make himself and everybody else miserable with his gloomy, long face; shows by his mental poise and calmness that he is master of the situation.

All fear is based upon the fact that the sufferer feels weak because of his consciousness of being separated from the Infinite Strength, Supply, and when he comes into consciousness of at-one-ment with the Power that made and sustains him, when he finds that peace which satisfies and which passeth all understanding — then will he feel a sense of the glory of being; and having once touched this power and tasted the infinite blessedness, he will never be content to roam again, never be satisfied with the flesh pots of Egypt.

It is a pitiful thing to see strong, vigorous men and women who have inherited God-like qualities and who bear the impress of divinity, going about the world full of all sorts of fears and terrors, with anxious, worried faces, as though life had been a perpetual disappointment. These are not the children God intended.

A millennium will come when fear in all its hideous forms of expression is eliminated. Then man will rise to the majesty of perfect confidence, of sublime self-faith; a consciousness of security and freedom of which he has never before dreamed, and his power and efficiency will be multiplied a hundredfold.

Our sense of fear or terror is always in proportion to our sense of weakness or inability to protect ourselves from the cause of it. When conscious of being stronger than that which terrorizes weaker persons, we have no sense of fear.

We are told that Hercules was not haunted by the fear of other men. The consciousness that he possessed superior power lifted him above anxiety or fear that others might injure him.

"There is a slave whose name is Fear,
     A trembling, cringing thing;
There is a king whose name is Will,
     And every inch a king."

IX. ONE WITH THE DIVINE

IX. ONE WITH THE DIVINE

The secret of all health, prosperity, and happiness is being in conscious union with the Divine.

T HE late Professor Shaler, of Harvard University, said that the greatest discovery of the last century was that of the unity of everything in the universe, the oneness of all life.

This idea that there is but one principle running through the universe, one life, one truth, one reality, that this power is divinely beneficent, and that we are in this great current principle, which is running Godward, is one of the most inspiring, encouraging, and fear-killing that ever entered the human mind.

Life will take on new meaning when we come into the realization of our at-one-ment with this great creative, sustaining principle of the universe.

The realization that in the truth of our being we are actually a part of this great principle, a necessary, *inseparable* part of it, and that we can no more be annihilated than can the laws of mathematics, that we must partake of all of the qualities which compose our Creator, that we must be perfect and immortal because we were created by Perfection, are a part of immortal Principle, solves the greatest mysteries of life and gives us a wonderful sense of security, safety, satisfaction, and contentment, which nothing else can give.

The constant contemplation of our union with the Infinite life, the realization that literally "I and my Father are one," helps to establish a certainty, an assurance that we are not the playthings of chance, the puppets of accident or fate, that we are not tossed hither and thither in the universe the victims of a cruel destiny which we can not control.

Just in proportion as we realize this oneness with the Divine, this at-one-ment with our Maker, do our lives become calm, confident, creative.

There is no doubt that St. Paul had a glimpse of the union of man with this great creative sustaining Principle when he said: "For I am persuaded that neither death, nor life, nor angels, nor principalities, nor powers, nor things present, nor things to come, nor height, nor depth, nor any other creature shall be able to separate us from the love of God."

" Ye shall know the truth (of your divinity) and the truth shall make you free," that is, free from the slavery of fear, anxiety, care, free from the bondage of superstition, uncertainty, and limitation, free from the thought of poverty and distress.

The coming man will lose all sense of fear because he will be conscious of his oneness with Omnipotent Power.

The art of all arts is to be so entrenched, so poised in principle, so anchored in faith in everybody and everything — faith in the final triumph of harmony, truth, and justice — and to be so centered in truth that *nothing* can possibly shake us or disturb our equilibrium.

I have seen a delicate woman pass through sufferings and trials which would have sent most strong men and women to an insane asylum, and yet she never wavered or complained, but was always, even during the darkest hours, poised, helpful, serene, kindly, always full of love for her fellow men. There was a light in her eye which was not born of earth, because she was so entrenched in principle, in truth, so conscious of her oneness with the Divine, so completely in tune with the Infinite, and her faith was so gigantic, that nothing could happen to throw her off her center. Not even torture or starvation, or ostracism, could snuff out that divine light which shone in her eyes, or destroy her equanimity or serenity. She felt the presence of a Divine hand leading, guiding, protecting her, and she was not afraid.

It has ever been a mystery to the world that martyrs and prisoners could go through such sufferings and tortures, not only without a tremor of fear, but even with the assurance of victorious triumph. The reason is that they were anchored in eternal principle, buttressed by truth, justice, and right. Nothing could happen seriously to disturb them, because the hand that held them fast was Omnipotent, Divine.

The mind that has once caught a glimpse of its at-one-ment with Divinity, that has felt in tune with the Infinite, is never again afraid of anything that can happen to it, because it knows the closing of one door may only mean the opening of another, perhaps to infinitely greater and grander opportunity.

The closer we are to Divinity, the nearer we are to the limitless source of things. When we feel strongest, when we feel conscious of the power which is back of the flesh, but not of it, when we feel that we are in touch with Divinity, our power is greater and our supply larger.

If we could only open ourselves without stint, without restraint, fully to this divine inflow of power, what forces our lives could and would become!

We are so weak and inefficient because we shut off this power by our wrong-thinking, our vicious-living. No man can be really strong while conscious of wrong-doing.

Every time a man does wrong he weakens himself by so much. In this way, many men cut themselves almost entirely off from their conscious divine connection by severing the strands, the cable of justice, truth, love, right, and are thus shorn of their power.

Much of our greatest dishonesty is with ourselves. Each wrong act cuts a strand in the cable which connects us with our God. This accounts for the cowardice of a criminal who was once a hero. He has cut himself loose from his Creator Father, and the consciousness of this separateness from the great principle which he inherited from Him gives him a sense of *isolation,* uncertainty, helplessness, and the feeling that he is no longer a complete man.

Every time we do wrong, every time we depart from the truth, every time we commit a dishonest, unworthy act, do a mean, contemptible thing, we lessen the Omnipotent grip upon us, and then we become a prey to all sorts of fears, apprehensions, dreads, and doubts. Separated from the Divine Power, we feel as helpless as a little child left alone in the dark.

Man is beginning to learn that his power, his success, his happiness are in proportion to the completeness of his consciousness of this divine connection, and that he is mighty or weak as he keeps it inviolate and sacred, or breaks it.

All our troubles come from our sense of separateness from the Infinite Source.

The moment we feel conscious that our union with the Great Source of things is broken, we are filled with uncertainty and apprehension; we feel a sense of helplessness, which makes us weak, timid, apprehensive. Fear, anxiety, worry, are positive evidence that we have lost our divine connection and strayed from home, that we are out of tune with the Infinite, and in discord with principle.

Our strength comes from the conscious oneness with Omnipotence.

Perfect love casteth out fear, because perfect love annihilates all the idea of separateness between ourselves and Infinite love.

When we sense our at-one-ment with Him, when we become fully conscious of this divine reunion, all of our troubles flee, all of our diseases and our sins are healed.

When we are in such close contact with Deity that we actually feel God (good) all sense of weakness, limitation, fatigue, timidity, doubt, will vanish, and we shall have that perfect fearlessness which comes from the consciousness of our at-one-ment with Truth.

The nearer man approaches to the recognition of this union, he expresses in his being the principles of life, of truth, of beauty, everything that builds, that is constructive, creative, and the farther he is from all that is destructive —the deadly, the discordant.

The moment we become thoroughly conscious that we are connected with this Divine current running heavenward, the great underlying Principle of the universe, that we are a part of the great Truth, we take on new power, our courage and confidence multiply our ability.

Man is great in proportion as he reflects truth, justice, right. He is a weakling, a nobody when he depends upon his own power and does not recognize this divinity principle.

No man can attain to the maximum of his power until he recognizes that he is a part of the great Principle of the universe.

"The Divinity that shapes our ends is in ourselves, it is our very self."

The very holding of the thought that we are truth itself, that error is abnormal to us, that we are harmony and not discord, that we are the principle of life, the very essence of love, justice, truth, beauty, gives us peace, serenity, a steadfastness and spiritual uplift which no material things can bestow.

Just in proportion as we have perfect connection, are at-one-ment with the Divine, shall we receive the life current, the health current which can heal all our diseases. This is the secret of all healing, of all health, prosperity, and happiness, — the *conscious union with the Divine*. There is no harmony, no health, no genuine happiness that is lasting and worth while outside of this at-one-ment. If we could only constantly live in the consciousness of it, we could always maintain physical and mental harmony. This is the secret of all human blessedness.

In this consciousness we do not grow old. Instead of declining with the years, we perpetually renew our youth, and constantly advance to greater and greater blessedness. Nothing can sever our Divine connection, separate us from God (good) except sin. In so far as we depart from the qualities which make up divinity and which we have inherited, — such as justice, truth, harmony, love, — just so far do we break our connection with the current running God-ward.

What a comforting and sustaining thought it is that an Infinite power presides over us which is kinder to us than we are to ourselves, kinder than we can be to those we love best; a force which is always ready to heal our hurts and to restore us, no matter how we have sinned in violating nature's law!

When one feels that his hand is gripped by the Omnipotent hand he is "too near to God for doubt or fear" and he knows that no harm can come to him from any finite source. To feel that we are held always, everywhere, by this Divine hand and protected by Omnipotent Wisdom steadies the life wonderfully and gives a poise and confidence that nothing else can.

The realization of all this will help us to live the life worth while, and will show us the barrenness, the hollowness, the emptiness of the selfish, greedy struggle in which most of us are engaged. The consciousness that we *actually do live, move, and have our being in Divinity* will elevate our standards and multiply our powers marvelously.

A piece of well-magnetized steel will lift another, unmagnetized, eight times its own weight. A man in touch with the Divine Principle, magnetized by the consciousness of his oneness with the great creative force of the universe, in touch with Omnipotence has many times the power of the man who depends upon his own puny strength. In comparison they are like a motorman who puts up his trolley pole and draws from the great wire the help of the mighty electrical current, and one who tries to push his car by his own strength.

"Let the mind be in you which was also in Christ," that is, the mind that gives health, peace, and happiness; the thought that gives harmony, justice, truth, and beauty. This is impossible unless we live, move and have our very being in Him, unless we abide under the shadow of the Almighty.

The very idea of persistently holding the thought that one is divinely upheld, the thought that no harm can possibly come to him while he is thus ensconced in the Divine Presence destroys all fear and worry; restores confidence, and multiplies power.

X. GETTING IN TUNE

X. GETTING IN TUNE

If we could only learn the art of always keeping ourselves in harmony we could multiply our effectiveness immeasurably.

OTHING could induce Ole Bull to play in public until his violin was in perfect tune. It did not make any difference how long it took him or how uneasy his audience became, if a string stretched the least bit during a performance, even though the discord was not noticed by any one but himself, the instrument had to be put into harmony before he went on. A poorer musician would not be so particular. He would say to himself, " I will run through this piece no matter if one string is down a bit. No one may detect it but myself."

Great music teachers say that nothing will ruin the sensitiveness of the ear and lower the musical perception and standard so quickly as using an instrument out of tune or singing with others who can not appreciate fine tone distinctions. The mind after a while ceases to distinguish delicate shadings of tone. The voice quickly imitates and follows the musical instrument accompanying it. The ear is deceived, and, very soon, the singer forms the habit of singing off key.

It does not matter what particular instrument you may be using in the great life orchestra, whether it be the violin, the piano, the voice, or your mind expressing itself in literature, law, medicine, or any other vocation, you can not afford to start your concert, with the great human race for your audience, without getting it in tune.

Whatever else you may do, do not play out of tune, sing out of tune, or work out of tune. Do not let your discordant instrument spoil your ear or your mental appreciation. Familiarity with discord will wreck your success perceptions. Not even a Paderewski could win exquisite harmonies from a piano out of tune.

Mental discord is fatal to quality in work. The destructive emotions — worry, anxiety, hatred, jealousy, anger, greed, selfishness, are all deadly enemies of efficiency. A man can no more do his best work when possessed by any of these emotions than a watch can keep good time when there is friction in the bearings of its delicate mechanism. In order to keep perfect time the watch must be exquisitely adjusted. Every wheel, every cog, every bearing, every jewel must be mechanically perfect, for any defect, any trouble, any friction anywhere will make absolutely correct time impossible. The human machinery is infinitely more delicate than the mechanism of the finest chronometer and it needs regulating, needs to be put in perfect tune, adjusted to a nicety every morning before it starts on the day's run, just as a violin needs tuning before the concert begins.

Have you ever watched a centrifugal wringer in a laundry? It wabbles so badly when it first begins to revolve that it seems as though it would tear itself to pieces, but gradually, as the velocity increases, the motion becomes steadier and steadier, and the machine speeds with lightning rapidity on its center. When it once gains its perfect balance nothing seems to disturb it, although when it first began to revolve the least thing made it wabble.

A thousand and one trifles which disturb one who has not found his mental center do not affect the poised, self-centered soul at all. Even great things, panics, crises, failures, fires, the loss of property or friends, disasters of any kind, do not throw him off his balance. He has found his center, his equilibrium, and no longer vacillates between hope and despair. He has found that he is a part of the great unity law that runs all through the universe, a part of the Infinite Idea.

A poised, balanced mind unifies all the mental energies of the system, while the mind that flies all to pieces at the least provocation is constantly demoralized; the mental forces are scattered, there is a lack of coordination, mental cohesion, and consequent power.

Harmony is the secret of all effectiveness, beauty, happiness; and harmony is simply keeping ourselves in tune with the Infinite.

This means absolute health of all the mental and moral faculties. Poise, serenity, amiability, sweetness of temper tend to keep the whole mental and physical economy in harmony with the perpetual renewal processes constantly going on within us, which are destroyed by friction.

Man is like a wireless telegraph. He is constantly sending out messages of peace and power, of harmony or of discord, according to the character of the thought, the ideal. These messages are flying from us with lightning speed in every direction, and they arouse in others qualities like themselves.

The poised soul is so intrenched in the calm

of eternal harmony that he is beyond the reach of disaster or the fear of it, conscious that he so rests in the great arms of Infinite love and perfection that nothing can harm him, because he lives, moves, and has his being in eternal truth. Such a great serene soul is like a huge iceberg, balanced by the calm in the depths of the sea. It laughs at the giant waves which beat against its sides and the storms which lash it. They do not even cause it a tremor; because its huge bulk which enables it to ride calmly and serenely without perturbation when lashed by the ocean fury is poised in the perpetual calm in the depths below.

It is strange that men who are very shrewd in other matters should be so shortsighted, so ignorant, so utterly foolish in regard to the importance of keeping their marvelous, intricate, and delicate mental machinery every day in tune. Many a business man drags himself wearily through a discordant day, and finds himself completely exhausted at night, who would have accomplished a great deal more with infinitely less effort, and have gone home in a much fresher condition, if he had taken a little time to put himself in tune before going to his office in the morning.

The man who goes to work in the morning feeling out of sorts with everybody, in an antagonistic attitude of mind toward life and especially toward those with whom he has to deal, is in no condition to bring the maximum of his power to his task. A large percentage of his mental force will not be available.

People who have never tried it can not begin to realize the tremendous advantage of putting oneself in tune in the morning before starting on the day's work.

A New York business man recently told me that he never allows himself to go to his office in the morning until he has put his mind into perfect harmony with the world. If he has the slightest feeling of envy or jealousy, if he feels that he is selfish or unfair, if he has not the right attitude toward his partner or any of his employees, he simply will not go to work until his instrument is in tune, until his mind is clear of any form of discord. He says he has discovered that if he starts out in the morning with a right attitude of mind toward everybody, he gets infinitely more out of the day than he otherwise would; that whenever he has allowed himself to go to work in the past in a discordant condition he has not obtained nearly as good results and he has made those about him unhappy, to say nothing of the increased wear and tear upon himself.

One reason why the lives of so many men are thin, lean, and ineffective is because they do not rise above the things that untune their minds, irritate, annoy and worry them, and produce discord.

Many of these people who do only mediocre things really have a great deal of ability, but are so sensitive to friction that they can not do effective work. If they only had some one to steer them, to plan for them, to keep discord away from them and to help them keep in harmony, they could do remarkable things. Yet those who do great things are obliged to acquire this " art of arts " for themselves. No one can exercise it for them, and no one can accomplish anything very great in this world unless he is able to rise superior to the thousand and one things which would irritate and distract his attention.

A great many people who are disagreeable and irritable when they are tired are very amiable and harmonious when they are rested. This ought to show them that the cause of their irritability and inharmony is due to the sin of tired nerves and brain exhaustion.

How often we see men who have become

absolutely unbearable, after a year of hard work, completely revolutionized when they return from a trip abroad or a few weeks' vacation in the country! They do not seem like the same men that they were before they went away. The trifles which would throw them into a fit of passion before their vacation do not affect them at all now.

The mechanism of the mind is extremely delicate, and any of the animal passions let loose in the mental realm create fearful havoc in a very short time.

As a squeaking axle indicates the want of a lubricant, so friction or discord anywhere in the physical economy is a warning that something is wrong. It is not normal that the beautiful and delicate machinery which God finished and pronounced " good " should be out of repair. A dispute at the breakfast table, or any little wrangling in the morning may destroy the peace of the household for the entire day. A moment's hot temper may cost you a very dear friendship for life.

How little we appreciate the marvelousness of this exquisite mechanism of the mind which forms the connecting link between the created and the Creator! It is through this that a human being is linked to the Divine. Instead of giving thanks and supreme gratitude to our Maker every day for this *wonder of wonders* of the human brain — the mind — we abuse it in such a way that we do not get out of it a tithe of what we might.

We run through this exquisite mechanism the coarsest, most vicious, destructive thought. We force it to do work when it is jaded and out of tune; when its spontaneity is gone, and its vital standards are low; force it by all sorts of stimulants and will-power. We strain its exquisite gossamer mechanism until it is often prematurely injured, overstrained, ruined for its finest work.

It was intended as an instrument of a happiness so superb, an existence so grand and sublime, as we, in our coarse, clumsy, brutal way of treating it, have no conception of. The right use of the mind would soon bring the millennium.

We ought to so school ourselves that no matter what happens we should not lose our presence of mind, our balance. We should always keep our equilibrium so as to be able, no matter what happens, to do the level-headed thing, the wise thing, the right, square thing.

How many men have failed to achieve the great success which their ability prophesied because of the "touchy" habit, the scolding, fretting, nagging habit!

Somewhere in my travels I have seen what appeared to be a great stone face carved out of the side of a huge cliff, a face scarred and scratched by the sharp edge of gravel and sand hurled against it during the tremendous sand storms of the desert. Everywhere we see human faces scratched and scarred by tempests of passion, of anger, by chafing, fretting and worrying until the divine image is almost erased, and all power of accomplishing effective work has been destroyed.

How little we realize the power there is in harmony! It makes all the difference in the world in our life-work whether we are balanced and serene, or are continually wrought up, full of discords and errors, and harassed with all sorts of perplexing, vicious things.

If we could only learn the art of keeping ourselves in harmony, we could multiply our effectiveness many times and add years to our lives. A man feels like a giant when his mind is perfectly poised, when his mental processes are running smoothly and nothing is troubling him. On the other hand, gravel in the shoe would make a Webster a fourth-rate orator. I have seen a great statesman shorn of his power and

made perfectly miserable by gnats and mos-
quitoes. He could not think. He could not
use half of his great mental powers. It took
all of his time to fight these little pests.

The efficiency of a great majority of business and professional men is seriously marred
by little irritating annoyances.

No human being can express the best thing
in him until he is in tune with the Infinite, until
his purpose lies parallel with that of his God.
While there is divergence, while there is fight-
ing between one's own plan and the purpose
which God has marked in one's very constitution, the work must be inferior. As long as
we are working at cross-purposes with our
Creator's plan, there can be no worthy achievement.

Those who would attain exquisite mental
poise must dive into the depths of their beings,
where there is eternal calm which no mental
tempest can disturb, — a calm in which the
mind is in communication with the Divine.
Dwelling upon human qualities will never
bring perfect mental balance, that divine
serenity which makes mere physical beauty
unattractive in comparison.

Some of our best observatories are built upon
mountain tops so that the great lens which

sweeps the heavens may not be obscured by the dust, the dirt, the mists floating in the lower atmosphere. In order to shut out the din, the noises which distract the mind, in order to shut out the thousand and one disturbing influences in our strenuous life, the things which warp and twist and distort us, it is necessary to rise into the higher realm of thought and feeling, where we can breathe a purer air, get in closer touch with the Divine.

We shall be satisfied when we awake in His likeness, and when we wake in His likeness we wake in our own, because we were created in His likeness.

Why should we not have divine power if we are of divine origin? Why think it so strange for us to partake of the attributes of our Maker? Do you expect your child to be an inferior being to yourself, not to partake of any of your power or your higher attributes?

Why should God's offspring think it strange that what is in God is in him?

The trouble with us is that we do not understand the principle of availing ourselves of the Divine Power, and until we do we shall always work at a disadvantage, doing little things with great effort when we might do grand things easily.

What makes human beings so restless, discontented and unhappy is that they have lost their bearings, their divine connection. Like a child which has lost its mother, the soul is ever seeking its God and never will be free from fear, never have the consciousness of security and assurance of protection, until it has found Him.

When you get into peaceful at-one-ment with the One Life, feel that you are drawing to yourself every good thing from the inexhaustible supply, you know that all of the yearnings and longings of your heart can thus be realized. Here is where the creative process goes on. From this invisible supply we can draw realities to match our desires.

We know that when we put ourselves into harmony with this great creative, beneficient power which healeth all our hurts and diseases, we not only unfold all our faculties harmoniously, but also are conscious of a marvelous happiness, a peace of mind which ought to convince us of the kindliness of this divine force.

Conscious cooperation with the creative force of the universe will bring man into complete realization of peace, power, and plenty, the blessedness that is his birthright.

XI. THE GREAT WITHIN

XI. THE GREAT WITHIN

There is a Power inside of you which if you could discover and use would make of you everything you ever dreamed or imagined you could become.

The same Power that created us sustains and repairs us, and this Power is right inside of us.

HAVE seen a man of ordinary strength, hypnotized and suspended by head and ankles on the edges of two chairs, support half a dozen or more heavy men on his body. Sometimes a horse is thus supported on a see-saw board placed across the subject's body.

These are mostly mental feats, because a man of average strength could no more sustain a twelve-hundred-pound horse or half-a-dozen heavy men on his body thus suspended than he could fly without a machine. He could not be made to believe that he could do such a thing. Yet while under the powerful suggestion of a hypnotist that he *can* do it, he does it easily.

Now, from whence came the power which enabled the subject to do this marvelous thing? Certainly not from the hypnotist, for he merely called it out of the subject; it did not come from space outside of him. It was latent *in the man himself.*

Such experiments give us glimpses of enormous powers within us about which we know very little, and which, if we could use, would enable us to do marvelous things.

Without being able to define it, we instinctively feel that there is a great power within us, a power beyond the human that is guiding us, a subconscious soul power which presides over our destinies and which lends us superhuman aid when we make a great call upon it in danger or an emergency, a desperate strait, or when in great stress in prayer.

It is this soul power which makes a giant out of an invalid in an instant's time when the house takes fire or some great catastrophe occurs, when a child, dearer to the mother than life, is in imminent danger. There are many instances where very delicate invalids, who were not supposed to be able to sit up, have, in a fire or some other great danger or emergency, done that which under ordinary circumstances would have been difficult even for the strongest men to do.

From whence came this power, almost within the twinkling of an eye? It came from

the Great Within, and these instances reveal
— as the falling apple did to Newton — a wonderful law. They make it certain that we all
possess marvelous, unused powers.

The new philosophy is trying to show people
how to discover and utilize the wonderful
powers in the Great Within of themselves
which they have hitherto been unable to use,
or except in a very limited way.

There are powers inside of you, which if
you could discover and use, *would make of you
everything you ever dreamed or imagined you
could become.*

If we only knew what tremendous forces are
locked up inside of us, we should not be so
surprised when a tramp or a hobo becomes
transformed into a hero almost in an instant,
in some great railroad wreck, or fire, or other
emergency. The hero was there all the time;
the catastrophe simply revealed it.

We none of us know what wonderful things
we could do if an emergency great enough,
imperative enough, were to make a sudden
call upon us.

*It is from this Great Within that the power
comes which does immortal deeds.* We are
conscious that there is something in us but
not of us which is never sick, never tired, which

never goes wrong. All principle, truth, love, live in this Great Within. Here is the home of beauty and justice. Here is where spiritual beauty dwells. Here abides " the peace which passeth all understanding," and here shines " the light that was never on sea or land."

We are all conscious of something within us that is deathless, something immortal, divine. We all feel this, the living Christ, this silent messenger which accompanies us through life, trying to warn us, advise us, protect us, no matter where we go, or how low we fall.

Many feel just as sure of this blessed mothering Presence, this messenger of peace and good-will, as though they could see Him with their eyes.

There is something in the Great Within of us that tells us we are at one with the power that made all things and that we shall sometime, somewhere, come into at-one-ment with this power, that when we have once drunk at this great fountain-head, we shall never know thirst or want again.

Many people pass out of this plane of consciousness with enough health latent in the billions of cells in the body to restore them to life, if it could only be aroused. There are cases in medical history where patients have been apparently restored to life, even at the moment of impending dissolution, by a relative or a physician calling to them imperatively, vehemently, to return to life. But generally the victim's conviction that he can not get well and that he *must* die paralyzes and destroys the disease-resisting power of the body, so that there is nothing to check the malady, which may be fatal only because of the loss of faith and the patient's conviction that he can not recover.

In the same way there are multitudes of shiftless people, in the great failure army to-day, with scarcely energy enough to keep them alive, who have forces slumbering deep within themselves which, if they could only be awakened, would enable them to do wonderful things.

Most people have latent ability enough to accomplish wonders, but often only a fraction of this power is aroused; it lies dormant unless fired into action by some great inspiration, emergency, or by some life crisis which drives them to desperation, and forces them to make a supreme call upon their interior forces.

We are all surprised sometimes in our lives — through some great crisis or when in a desperate situation — to find that a tremendous reserve power comes to our assistance from somewhere; that from somewhere in the Great Within, from mysterious depths of our natures, come marvelous powers when the call is loud enough and strong enough, powers of which we may never before have been conscious.

The time will come when we shall be able to use at will all the latent potencies slumbering in the Great Within of us, which we get at so unconsciously in a great crisis or desperate situation but which at other times it seems impossible for us to reach.

One great trouble is that we do not have sufficient faith in the immense reserve power in our subconsciousness, and do not take proper means to arouse this slumbering power to action, although we sometimes see examples of the possibilities of great dynamic forces being aroused in people who never dreamed that they possessed them.

There is something in man that never deteriorates, never becomes demoralized or smirched, that is always true and always clean — the divine in him, the regenerative principle or force, which, if aroused, will work like a leaven in the life of the most depraved, until it brings that person back to his lost God (good), to his normal condition; and when a person is normal, he *wants* to do right, because he is built upon the principle of justice, honesty, and truth.

It is not normal for a man to go wrong. It is just as natural for a perfectly normal person to want to do right as it is for a flower to fling out its fragrance and beauty; the flower that is blighted and withholds its fragrance and beauty is abnormal.

It does not matter how far a human being may wander from the right, the divine something in him will sometime, somewhere, bring his whole life into absolute harmony; and that is heaven harmony.

If there is anything in this universe that is evident, it is that the Creator's plans are beneficent, and that human beings are constructed along the lines of right and justice, truth and virtue, and any deflections from these are abnormal.

A human being who is wicked, dishonest, greedy, or selfish is no more the man God made than discord is music.

Man must be in harmony with justice and truth and right because he is made to be just and true and right. That is his birthright. That is the divine in him.

This divinity in man will ultimately triumph.

It is just as certain as that truth will some-time triumph over error, that harmony will triumph over discord; for truth is the ever-lasting fact, and error, untruth, is not a fact; it is the absence of truth. Discord is not a fact; it is merely the absence of harmony, the great fact in the universe.

No friend was ever so unselfish, so true to us as is this great healing, beneficent life prin-ciple, this mysterious Power which created us and which maintains us, and we find that we are supported, sustained, in proportion to our conscious oneness with it.

The Power that created us is the same Power that makes us over new every night during sleep. It is the same Power that is constantly re-creating every cell in the body. "Je le ponsez et Dieu le guarit" (I dressed the wound and God healed it), was written by Ambroise Pare on the walls of the Ecole de Médicine at Paris.

"I am the Lord thy God (thy good), that healeth thee." Here is the secret of all cures. The Bible is full of accounts of mental healing. People who have never made a study of this phase of the healing philosophy would be sur-prised to find to what extent it is scattered all through the Scriptures.

"He forgiveth all thine iniquities and healeth all thy diseases."

"If a man keep My saying (that is, keep in His thoughts, the truth thought, the love thought), he shall never see death." (John 8:51).

How instinctively we turn to this Divine healing power when in trouble, when overwhelmed with sorrow and failure!

"Come unto Me all ye that labor and are heavy laden, and I will give you rest." Think what this invitation from the Almighty means! Peace that passeth understanding; immunity from all discords; freedom from all the enemies that have hitherto dogged our steps through life, blocking our progress, and destroying our happiness!

True prayer repairs the broken wires of our Divine connection, reassures us, brings us into harmony with the Infinite. This is the secret of all mental healing.

Think of the ridiculousness of any inert drug taken into the system competing with the immortal creative principle of all life! This creative principle does not inhere in any drug or any physical remedy. *Mind is the only creator. Nothing ever was or ever will be created or re-created except through mind.*

Only the Creator of the original tissues of our body can restore these tissues when diseased or destroyed.

In the final analysis all cures are self-cures, all healing is self-healing. The potency resides in the Great Within of us, in our God connection, in our oneness with Divinity. What a boon to the race, what a blessing to humanity if every one knew this one truth, that the only healing possible must come through the rousing of the recuperative, restorative forces *within himself,* and that this healing power is that which heals all his hurts and wounds, and which is perpetually renewing every cell in the body, and that it is the same power which created him, and keeps him alive every instant of his existence!

The coming physician will teach the patient that the creative processes are always going on within him, that the same power which has created him is in the perpetual act of re-creating, restoring him all his life, — as is shown the moment he breaks a bone or lacerates his flesh, when the healing processes begin immediately, — and if our education, prejudices, and convictions did not antagonize this creative process, but were trained to aid it, the healing would be quickly, perfectly done.

We are all conscious that there is a current deep within us that runs Godward, that this current carries unlimited supply. The poorest of us are in the very midst of plenty and in touch with Omnipotent Power, but we do not know it. If, with open mind and heart, we put ourselves in the success current, the current of good, of abundance, the supply will flow to us naturally, abundantly. The mind that is open to its inflow will never want.

It sometimes happens that men who purchase farms on the prairies find that some of their predecessors attempted to drive wells, and, failing to find water, sold out. But the more enterprising purchaser drills down deeper and strikes the living stream.

Multitudes of people go through life without ever going deep enough into their inner consciousness to strike the great living stream of supply. Hence, their lives are parched, dry, and unproductive. But if we dip deep enough into the Great Within of ourselves, we shall strike the stream of living water, of which, if we once drink, we shall never thirst, never lack, or want again.

We all have moments when we get glimpses of the great possibilities within ourselves. It may sometimes be an experience which takes away a loved one, which opens up a rift in our nature and gives us a glimpse of power which we never before knew we possessed. It may be the reading of an inspiring book, or an encouraging friend that gives us a glimpse of our possible selves, but, whatever it is, we are never quite the same again after we have once felt the thrill of power from the very source of things.

When man feels the mighty principle of truth, of justice pulsating through him, he knows that even with all the world against him he and this principle are a majority.

This was why Lincoln was such a power in the world. It was not merely what was in his brain; it was the mighty principle behind the man back of the flesh, it was Truth and Justice which acted through him, that made him such a power.

Lincoln was conscious that there was something inside of him, something back of him which was more than human, a power which carried divine authority, and that if he disobeyed it he would instantly be robbed of his power and peace of mind. He felt that truth and justice were speaking through him; that he was simply a medium.

Did you ever realize that you are a part of

the universal intelligence that underlies all things, the intelligence which furnishes the pattern for the rose before it pushes out into objective reality, the intelligence which shapes every flower and plant and tree and blade of grass, and that this great ocean of intelligent energy that fills the universe exists in the Great Within of you, is at your disposal to produce what you will?

One man shapes this intelligent activity into a statue which enchants mankind, another into an architectural wonder, another into a railroad, another into a telephone or sewing machine, another into hideous forms which contaminate and demoralize every beholder.

The one great Mind which pervades the universe originates every flower pattern, every tree, every animal, every living thing. It is from this same mind, this power in the Great Within of us, that we create everything which goes to make up our life.

If man could only harmonize with the Divine Principle within, the Principle which never dies, which is never sick and never sins, he could reach his greatest efficiency, his highest state of blessedness.

Most people do not half realize how sacred a thing a legitimate ambition is. What is this eternal urge within us which is trying to push us on and on, up and up? It is the God urge, the God push in the Great Within of us, which is perpetually prodding us to do our best, and bids us refuse to accept our second best.

When we come into the realization of that great, silent, vital energy within us which is able to satisfy all the soul's desires, all its yearnings, we shall no longer hunger or thirst, for all the good things of the universe will be ours. No life can be poor when enfolded in the Infinite Arms, and living in the very midst of abundance, the source of all supply.

XII. A NEW WAY OF BRINGING UP CHILDREN

XII. A NEW WAY OF BRINGING UP CHILDREN

Only a thought, but the work it wrought
Could never by tongue or pen be taught,
But it ran through a life like a thread of gold,
And the life bore fruit a hundredfold."

OT long ago there was on exhibition in New York a young horse which can do most marvelous things; and yet his trainer says that only five years ago he had a very bad disposition. He was fractious, and would kick and bite, but now instead of displaying his former viciousness, he is obedient, tractable, and affectionate. He can readily count and reckon up figures, can spell many words, and knows what they mean.

In fact this horse seems to be capable of learning almost anything. Five years of kindness have completely transformed the vicious yearling colt. He is very responsive to kindness, but one can do nothing with him by whipping or scolding him. His trainer says that in all the five years he has never touched him with a whip but once.

I know a mother of a large family of children who has never whipped but one of them, and that one only once.

When her first child was born people said she was too good-natured to bring up children, that she would spoil them, as she would not correct or discipline them, and would do nothing but love them. But this love has proved the great magnet which has held the family together in a marvelous way. Not one of those children has gone astray. They have all grown up manly and womanly, and love has been wonderfully developed in their natures. Their own affection responded to the mother's love and has become their strongest motive. To-day all her children look upon " Mother " as the grandest figure in the world. She has brought out the best in them because she saw the best in them. The worst did not need correcting or repressing, because the expulsive power of a stronger affection drove out of the nature or discouraged the development of vicious tendencies which, in the absence of a great love, might have become dominant and ruined the life.

Love is a healer, a life-giver, a balm for our hurts. All through the Bible are passages which show the power of love as a healer and life-lengthener. " With long life will I satisfy him," said the Psalmist, " because he hath set his love upon me."

When shall we learn that the great curative principle is love, that love heals because it is harmony? There can be no discord where it reigns. Love is serenity, is peace and happiness.

Love is the great disciplinarian, the supreme harmonizer, the true peacemaker. It is the great balm for all that blights happiness or breeds discontent, a sovereign panacea for malice, revenge, and all the brutal propensities. As cruelty melts before kindness, so the evil passions find their antidote in sweet charity and loving sympathy.

The mother is the supreme shaper of life and destiny.

Many a mother's love for her children has undoubtedly stayed the ravages of some fatal disease. Her conviction that she was necessary to them and her great love for them have braced her, and have enabled her to successfully cope with the enemies of her life for a long time.

One mother I know seems to have the magical art of curing nearly all the ills of her children by love. If any member of the family has any disagreeable experience, is injured or pained, hurt or unhappy, he immediately goes to the mother for the universal balm, which heals all troubles.

This mother has a way of drawing the troubled child out of discord into the zone of perpetual harmony. If he is swayed by jealousy, hatred, or anger, she applies the love solvent, the natural antidote for these passion poisons. She knows that scolding a child when he is already suffering more than he can bear is like trying to put out a fire with kerosene.

Our orphan asylums give pathetic illustration of how quickly the child mind matures and ages prematurely without the uplift and enrichment of the mother love, the mother sympathy, — parental protection and home influence.

It is well known that children who lose their parents and are adopted by their grandparents and live in the country, where they do not have an opportunity to mingle much with other children, adopt the manners and mature vocabulary of their elders, for they are very imitative, and become little men and women before they are out of their youth.

Think of a child reared in the contaminating

atmosphere of the slums, where everything is dripping with suggestions of vulgarity and wickedness of every description! Think of his little mind being filled with profanity, obscenity, and filth of all kinds! Is it any wonder that he becomes so filled with vicious, criminal suggestions that he tends to become like his environment?

Contrast such a child with one that is brought up in an atmosphere of purity, refinement, and culture, and whose mind is always filled with noble, uplifting suggestions of the true, the beautiful, and the lovely. What a difference in the chances of these two children, and without any special effort or choice of their own! One mind is trained upward, towards the light, the other downward, towards darkness.

What chance has a child to lead a noble life when all his first impressionable years are saturated with the suggestion of evil, when jealousy and hatred, revenge, quarreling and bickering, all that is low and degrading, fill his ears and eyes?

How important it is that the child should only hear and see and be taught that which will make for beauty and for truth, for loveliness and grandeur of character!

We ought to have a great deal of charity for those whose early lives have been soaked in evil, criminal, impurity thoughts.

The minds of children are like the sensitive plates of a photographer, recording every thought or suggestion to which they are exposed. These early impressions make up the character and determine the future possibility.

If you would encourage your child and help him to make the most of himself, inject bright, hopeful, optimistic, unselfish pictures into his atmosphere. To stimulate and inspire his confidence and unselfishness means growth, success, and happiness for him in his future years, while the opposite practise may mean failure and misery.

It is of infinitely more importance to hold the right thought towards a child, the confident, successful, happy, optimistic thought, than to leave him a fortune without this. With his mind properly trained he could not fail, could not be unhappy, without reversing the whole formative process of his early life.

Keep the child's mind full of harmony, of truth, and there will be no room for discord, for error.

It is cruel constantly to remind children of their deficiencies or peculiarities. Sensitive children are often seriously injured by the suggestion of inferiority and the exaggeration of defects which might have been entirely over·come. This everlasting harping against the bad does not help the child half as much as keeping his little mind full of the good, the beautiful, and the true. The constant love suggestion, purity suggestion, nobility suggestion will so permeate the life after a while that there will be nothing to attract the opposite. It will be so full of sunshine, so full of beauty and love, that there will be little or no place for their opposites.

The child's self-confidence should be buttressed, braced, and encouraged in every possible way; not that he should be taught to overestimate his ability and his possibilities, but the idea that he is God's child, that he is heir to an Infinite inheritance, magnificent possibilities, should be instilled into the very marrow of his being.

A great many boys, especially those who are naturally sensitive, shy, and timid, are apt to suspect that they lack the ability which others have. It is characteristic of such youths that they distrust their own ability and are very easily discouraged or encouraged. It is a sin to shake or destroy a child's self-confidence, to reflect upon his ability or to suggest that he will never amount to much. These discouraging words, like initials cut in the sapling, grow wider and wider with the years, until they become great ugly scars in the man.

Most parents do not half realize how impressionable children are, and how easily they may be injured or ruined by discouragement or ridicule. Children require a great deal of appreciation, praise, and encouragement. They live upon it. It is a great tonic to them. On the other hand, they wither very quickly under criticism, blame, or depreciation. Their sensitive natures can not stand it. It is the worst kind of policy to be constantly blaming, chiding them, and positively cruel, bordering on criminality even, to suggest to them that they are mentally deficient or peculiar, that they are stupid and dull, and that they will probably never amount to anything in the world.

How easy it is for a parent or teacher to ruin a child's constructive ability, to change a naturally, positive creative mind to a negative, non-producing one, by chilling the child's enthusiasm, by projecting into his plastic mind the idea that he is stupid, dull, lazy, a " blockhead " and good-for-nothing; that he will never amount to anything; that it is foolish for him to try to be much, because he has not the ability or physical stamina to enable him to accomplish what many others do. Such teaching would undermine the brightest intellect.

I have known of an extremely sensitive, timid boy who had a great deal of natural ability, but who developed very slowly, whose whole future was nearly ruined by his teacher and parents constantly telling him that he was stupid and dull, and that he probably never would amount to anything. A little praise, a little encouragement, would have made a superb man of this youth, because he had the material for the making of one. But he actually believed that he was not up to the ordinary mental standard; he was thoroughly convinced that he was mentally deficient, and this conviction never entirely left him.

We are beginning to discover that it is much easier to attract than to coerce. Praise and encouragement will do infinitely more for children than threats and punishment. The warm sunshine is more than a match for the cold, has infinitely more influence in developing the bud, the blossom, and the fruit than the wind and the tempest, which suppress what responds voluntarily to the genial influence of the sun's rays.

We all know how boys will work like troopers under the stimulus of encouragement and praise. Many parents and teachers know this, and how fatal the opposite policy is. But unfortunately a great majority do not appreciate the magic of praise and appreciation.

Pupils will do anything for a teacher who is always kind, considerate, and interested in them; but a cross, fractious, nagging one so arouses their antagonism that it often proves a fatal bar to their progress. There must be no obstruction, no ill-feeling between the teacher and the pupil, if the best results are to be obtained.

Many parents are very much distressed by the waywardness of their children; but this waywardness is often more imaginary than real. A large part of children's pranks and mischief is merely the outcome of exuberant youthful spirits, which must have an outlet, and if they are suppressed, their growth is fatally stunted. They are so full of life, energy, and so buoyant that they can not keep still. They *must* do *something*. Give them an outlet for their animal spirits. Love is the only power that can regulate and control them.

Do not try to make men of your boys or women of your girls. It is not natural. Love them.   Make home just as happy a place as possible, and give them rein, freedom.   Encourage them in their play, for they are now in their fun age.   Many parents ruin the larger, completer, fuller development of their children by repressing them, destroying their childhood, their play days, by trying to make them adults.   There is nothing sadder in American life than the child who has been robbed of its childhood.

Children are little animals, sometimes selfish, often cruel, due to the fact that some parts of their brain develop faster than others, so that their minds are temporarily thrown out of balance, sometimes even to cruel or criminal tendencies, but later the mind becomes more symmetrical and the vicious tendencies usually disappear.   Their moral faculties and sense of responsibility unfold more slowly than other traits, and, of course, they will do mischievous things; but it is a fatal mistake to be always suppressing them.   They must give out their surplus energy in some way. Encourage them to romp.   Play with them. It will keep you young, and will link them to you with hooks of steel.   Do not be afraid of losing your dignity.   If you make home the happiest, most cheerful place on earth for your children, if you love them enough, there is little danger of their becoming bad.

Thousands of parents by being so severe with their children, scolding and criticizing them and crushing their childhood, make them secretive and deceitful instead of open and transparent, and estrange them and drive them away from home.

A man ought to look back upon the home of his childhood as the Eden of his life, where love reigned, instead of as a place where a long-faced severity and harshness ruled, where he was suppressed and his fun-loving spirits snuffed out.

Every mother, whether she realizes it or not, is constantly using the power of suggestion in rearing her children, healing all their little hurts. She kisses the bumps and bruises and tells the child all is well again, and he is not only comforted, but really believes that the kiss and caress have magic to cure the injury. The mother is constantly antidoting and neutralizing the child's little troubles and discords by giving the opposite thought and applying the love-elixir.

It is possible, through the power of suggestion, to develop in children faculties upon which health, success, and happiness depend.

Most of us know how dependent our efficiency is upon our moods, our courage, hope. If the cheerful, optimistic faculties were brought out and largely developed in childhood, it would change our whole outlook upon life, and we would not drag through years of half-heartedness, discouragement, and mental anguish, our steps dogged by fear, apprehension, anxiety, and disappointment.

One reason why we have such poor health is because we have been steeped in poor-health thought from infancy. We have been saturated with the idea that pain, physical suffering, and disease are a part of life; necessary evils which can not be avoided. We have had it so instilled into us that robust health is the exception and could not be expected to be the rule that we have come to accept this unfortunate condition of things as a sort of fate from which we can not hope to get away.

The child hears so much sick talk, is cautioned so much about the dangers of catching all sorts of diseases, that he grows up with the conviction that physical discords, aches, pains, all discomfort and suffering, are a necessary part of his existence, that at any time disease is liable to overtake him and ruin his happiness and thwart his career.

Think of what the opposite training would do for the child; if he were taught that health is the everlasting fact and that disease is but the manifestation of the absence of harmony! Think what it would mean to him if he were trained to believe that abounding health, rich, full, complete, instead of sickness, that certainty instead of uncertainty were his birthright! Think what it would mean for him to *expect* this during all his growing years, instead of building into his consciousness the opposite, instead of being saturated with the sick thought and constantly being cautioned against disease and the danger of contracting it!

The child should be taught that God never created disease, and never intended that we should suffer; that we were made for abounding health and happiness, made for enjoyment not for pain — made to be happy, not miserable, to express harmony, not discord.

Children are extremely credulous. They are inclined to believe everything that an adult tells them, especially the nurse, the father and mother, and their older brothers and sisters. Even the things that are told them in jest they take very seriously; and their imaginations are so vivid and their little minds so impressionable that they magnify everything. They are often punished for telling falsehoods, when the fault is really due to their excessively active imagination.

Many ignorant or thoughtless parents and nurses constantly use fear as a means of governing children. They fill their little minds full of all sorts of fear stories and terror pictures which may mar their whole lives. They often buy soothing syrups and all sorts of sleeping potions to prevent the little ones from disturbing their rest at night, or to keep them quiet and from annoying them in the day time, and thus are liable to stunt their brain development.

Even if children were not seriously injured by fear, it would be wicked to frighten them, for it is wrong to deceive them. If there is anything in the world that is sacred to the parent or teacher, it is the unquestioned confidence of children.

I believe that the beginnings of deterioration in a great many people who go wrong could be traced to the forfeiting of the children's respect and confidence by the parents and teachers. We all know from experience that confidence once shaken is almost never entirely restored. Even when we forgive, we seldom forget; the suspicion often remains. There should never be any shadows between the child and his parents and teachers. He should always be treated with the utmost frankness, transparency, sincerity. The child's respect is worth everything to his parents. Nothing should induce them to violate it or to shake it. It should be regarded as a very sacred thing, a most precious possession.

Think of the shock which must come to a child when he grows up and discovers that those he has trusted implicitly and who seemed almost like gods to him have been deceiving him for years in all sorts of ways!

I have heard mothers say that they dreaded to have their children grow up and discover how they had deceived them all through their childhood; to have them discover that they had resorted to fear, superstition, and all sorts of deceits in order to govern or influence them.

Whenever you are tempted to deceive a child again, remember that the time will come when *he will understand,* and that he will receive a terrible shock when he discovers that you, up to whom he has looked with such implicit trust, such simple confidence, have deceived him.

Parents should remember that every distressing, blood-curdling story told to a child, every superstitious fear instilled into his young life, the mental attitude they bear towards him, the whole treatment they accord him, are making phonographic records in his nature which will be reproduced with scientific exactness in his future life.

Whatever you do, never punish a child when he is suffering with fear. It is a cruel thing to punish children the way most mothers and teachers do, anyway; but to punish a child when he is already quivering with terror is extremely distressing, and to whip a child when you are angry is brutal. Many children never quite forget or forgive a parent or teacher for this cruelty.

Parents, teachers, friends often put a serious stumbling-block in the way of a youth by suggesting that he ought to study for the ministry, or the law; to be a physician, an engineer, or enter some other profession or business for which he may be totally unfitted.

I know a man whose career was nearly ruined by the suggestion of his grandmother when he was a child that she would educate him for the church, and that it was her wish for him to become a clergyman.

It was not that she saw in the little child

any fitness for this holy office, but because *she wanted a clergyman in the family*, and she often reminded him that he must not disappoint her. The boy, who idolized his grandmother, pondered this thought until he became a young man. The idea possessed him so strongly that every time he tried to make a choice of a career the picture of a clergyman rushed first to his mind, and, although he could see no real reason why he should become a clergyman, the suggestion that he ought to worked like leaven in his nature and kept him from making any other choice until too late to enable him to succeed to any great extent.

I know a most brilliant and marvelously fascinating woman who is extremely ambitious to make a name for herself, but she is almost totally lacking in her ability to apply herself, even in the line where her talent is greatly marked. She seems to be abundantly endowed in every faculty and quality except this. Now, if her parents had known the secret of correcting mental deficiencies, building up weak faculties, this girl could have been so trained that she would probably have had a great career and made a world-wide name for herself.

I have in mind another woman, a most bril-

liant linguist, who speaks fluently seven lan-
guages. She is a most fascinating conversationalist and impresses one as having read
everything, but, although in good health, she
is an object of charity to-day, simply because
she has never developed her practical faculties
at all, and this because she was never trained
to work, to depend upon herself even in little
things when she was a child. She was fond of
her books, was a most brilliant scholar, but
never learned to be practical or to do anything herself. Her self-reliance and independence were never developed. All of her
early friends predicted a brilliant future for
her, but because of the very consciousness
of possessing so many brilliant qualities and
of the fact that she was flattered during all
her student life and not obliged to depend upon
herself for anything, she continued to exercise
her strong scholarship faculties only, little
dreaming that the neglect to develop her
weaker ones would wreck her usefulness and
her happiness.

It is not enough to possess ability. We
must be able to use it effectively, and whatever
interferes with its activity to that extent kills
efficiency. There are many people who are
very able in most qualities and yet their real

work is seriously injured and often practically ruined, or they are thrown into the mediocre class, owing to some weakness or deficiency which might have been entirely remedied by cultivation and proper training in earlier life.

I know a man of superb ability in nearly every respect who is so timid and shy that he does not dare push himself forward or put himself in the position of greatest advantage, does not dare *begin* things. Consequently his whole life has been seriously handicapped.

If children could only be taught to develop a positive, creative mind, it would be of infinitely more value and importance to them than inheriting a fortune with a non-productive one. Youths should be taught that the most valuable thing to learn in life next to integrity is how to build their minds up to the highest possible producing point, the highest possible state of *creative efficiency.*

The most important part of the education of the future will be to increase the chances of success in life and lessen the danger of failure and the wrecking of one's career by building up weak and deficient faculties, correcting one-sided tendencies, so that the individual will become more level-headed, better balanced, and have a more symmetrical mind.

Many students leave school and college knowing a great deal, but without a bit of improvement in their self-confidence, their initiative ability. They are just as timid, shy, and self-depreciatory as before entering.

Now, what advantage is it to send a youth out into the world with a head full of knowledge but without the confidence or assurance to use it effectively, or the ability to grapple with life's problems with that vigor and efficiency which alone can bring success?

It is an unpardonable reflection upon a college which turns out youths who dare not say their souls are their own, who have not developed a vigorous self-confidence, assurance, and initiative. Hundreds of students are turned out of our colleges every year who would almost faint away if they were suddenly called upon to speak in public, to read a resolution, or even to put a motion.

The time will come when an education will enable a youth while upon his feet in public to express himself forcefully, to use the ability he has and summon his knowledge quickly. He will be so trained in self-control, in self-confidence, in level-headedness, that he will not be thrown off his guard in an emergency. The future education will mean that what the student knows will be *available*, that he can utilize it at will, that he will be trained to use it *efficiently*.

Many of our graduates leave college every year as weak and inefficient in many respects as when they began their education. What is education for if it is not to train the youth to be the master of his faculties, master of every situation, able to summon all of his reserves of knowledge and power at will?

A college graduate, timid, stammering, blushing, and confused, when suddenly called upon to use his knowledge, whether in public or elsewhere, ought to be an unknown thing. Of what use is education which can not be summoned at will? Of what good are the reserves of learning which can not be marshaled quickly when we need them, which do not help one to be master of himself and the situation, whatever it may be?

The time will come when no child will be allowed to grow up without being taught to believe in himself, to have great confidence in his ability. This will be a most important part of his education, for if he believes in himself *enough*, he will not be likely to allow a single deficient faculty or weakness to wreck his career.

He should be reared in the conviction that he was sent into this world with a mission and that he is going to deliver it.

Every youth should be taught that it was intended he should fill a place in the world which no one else can fill; that he should expect to fill it, and train himself for it; taught that he was made in the Creator's image, that in the truth of his being he is divine, perfect, immortal, and that the image of God can not fail. He should be taught to think grandly of himself, to form a sublime estimate of his possibilities and of his future. This will increase his self-respect and self-development in well-proportioned living.

XIII. TRAINING FOR LONGEVITY

XIII. TRAINING FOR LONGEVITY

If the mind holds the old age pattern, the old age conviction, it will be out-pictured in the body.

If the mind holds the youthful pattern it will be faithfully copied in the body.

NE of the richest men in the United States says that he would give ten million dollars to prolong his life ten years. No doubt he would be willing to give a hundred millions.

How precious life is to all of us! It is a rare thing for even a criminal, the most dejected creature serving a life sentence, to wish to shorten his existence an hour if he could.

Whatever our ambition may be, nothing else can be quite so precious to most of us as life, and we want that life at its best. Every normal person dreads to see the marks of old age, the symptoms of decrepitude, and wants to remain fresh, buoyant, robust, as long as possible. Yet most people do not take sensible precautions to preserve their youth and vigor. They violate the health laws, longevity laws; sap their vitality in foolish, unnatural living, in deteriorating habits, and then wonder why their powers decline. Abused faculties and outraged nerves must pay the penalty. The long life is the controlled life.

If we took as much pains or made as great an effort to retain our youthfulness and our vigor as many of us do to make money, to amass a fortune, we could carry youth well-nigh to the century mark.

A man is like a fine clock, which, if properly cared for, will keep splendid time and run for a century, but which, if neglected or abused, will very soon get out of order, and wear out or give out long before it should.

It seems strange that although we all love life so dearly, cling to it with such desperate tenacity, we should sell it so cheaply, should deliberately throw away so many precious years, by wrong living and bad thinking.

As long as we go on thinking old age thoughts, harboring old age convictions, picturing old age characteristics, we shall continue to grow old. Our thoughts and our convictions will work against our real desires, just as our very effort, however strenuous it may be, to accumulate a fortune will be counteracted by our doubts and fears of failure.

The mental ideal determines what shall be built into the life, whether it shall be youthful or aging conditions. Every person has the inherent capacity for prolonging his life, increasing his potential longevity; but he must first understand the mental principle.

Perfect health, vigor, and robustness are impossible to one whose mind is a slave to the conviction that he is on the decline, that he is going down-hill physically, that his powers are gradually lessening through age.

The mind makes its own dead line. One's conviction places the limits.

Most people do not realize that their mental attitude is a positive energy which is constantly creating results. Every time we focus the mind, we are producing, creating something. If we focus it upon beauty, we are creating beauty. If we focus it upon the conditions of declining powers, of decrepitude, we help to create these conditions in the life. Any mental attitude which is adverse to the spirit of youth tends to produce hardening old age conditions.

If we live in mental youth, if we picture the processes of rejuvenation, of self-renewal, which are always going on in every cell of the body, the old age pictures can not be reproduced in it.

Many people assist rather than resist the

old age processes by giving in to them and harboring the conviction that they are getting along in years. They are always looking for signs of old age, the footprints of decline. The point of diminishing returns is a very tender spot to them. If they tire a little sooner than they once did, if they can not stand quite as much as when they were younger, they imagine that they have crossed the " dead line " placed by such men as Dr. Osler and others, and they begin to repeat tnat deadly saying, " I am not as young as I used to be."

I have a friend who is always referring to his age in such expressions as this: " You know, when a man gets past sixty he can't stand what he once could. I am beginning to feel pretty stiff, my bones are getting brittle, my muscles hard." He is always saying that he is too old for this, and too old for that. " Leave those things to young people," he will say, " they are not for men of my age." He is constantly dwelling upon his declining years, and keeping the picture of decrepitude in his mind.

" If at thirty or thirty-five you expect to become an old man or woman," said Prentice Mulford, " at fifty-five you will be one; because the mind makes the material correspond-ence of whatever it sets itself permanently upon. If you look forward to such decay of the body as a thing that must come, it will. People who keep young in their minds show it in the condition of their bodies. Three-fourths of our people look old at sixty, because they have always regarded it as an inevitable necessity that they must be on the down-hill side of life at that age."

One of the greatest delusions that ever crept into a mortal brain is that it is inevitable that a man at the age of forty or fifty should begin to lose his power and go down hill physically and mentally. Why should man, the grandest creation of God, begin to decline just as he is really beginning to get ready to live?

Man was made to come to his maximum of maturity, of power, of efficiency, and inward vision of wisdom relatively late in life. It is not a part of the Creator's plan that we become decrepit at fifty, sixty, or seventy, when we do not even come to full maturity until thirty. There is no analogy in the animal or the vegetable kingdom, no analogy anywhere in nature, to show that anything that takes so long to come to its maturity should decline so quickly. In fact, animals generally live from four to six times the length of their maturing period, and certainly the Creator's grandest work should not begin to reach decrepitude at only twice the years that it takes to mature. We should retain our vigor, our maximum of power, at least four times as long as it takes us to come to full maturity.

A man ought to be in the prime of his power and in the very zenith of his vigor at seventy-five.

Sir Herman Webber, the distinguished English physician, says that *most* people might easily live to be one hundred years of age.

The great accumulation of experience, of knowledge, of wisdom, gathered during the fruitful years of youth and middle age ought to enable a man who has lived normally to accomplish more in a single year in the seventies than in a half-dozen years in the twenties of life.

"I never could understand," says the poet Stedman, "why men consider seventy years a proper term of life. Five hundred years of earth are none too many — could we retain vigor and health. Wouldn't you like to be fifty years a traveler, fifty an inventor, fifty years a statesman — to practise painting, sculpture, — and all the time a fisher, sailor, poet, author, a man of the world? I should;

and then I might be willing to try some other sphere."

No one is old until the interest in life is gone out of him, until his spirit becomes aged, until his heart becomes cold and unresponsive; as long as he touches life at many points he can not grow old in spirit.

A man is old, no matter what his years, when he is out of touch with youth, with its ideals, its points of view, out of touch with the spirit of his times; when he has ceased to be progressive and up-to-date.

The idea that our energies and forces must begin to decline and the fires of ambition to die out after a certain age is reached has a most pernicious influence upon the mind. We do not realize how impossible it is for us to go beyond our self-placed " dead-line " limits, to do what we really believe we can not do.

We think ourselves into old age. Our convictions force us into it, and we shall go in that direction until we change our thought, until we turn completely about, reverse our attitude by reversing our thought, and face towards youth.

The conviction that we must grow old is ingrained in our very being, and we can not escape the ravages and marks of old age while we believe this condition is necessary and inevitable.

On the other hand, if we believe that the fundamental principle of life is founded in the God principle, and that that principle can not age, that time has no effect upon it, we shall be able to carry youth into age.

I believe that the conviction of old age, which is so thoroughly ground into our very existence, cuts off a great many precious years.

If we dwell upon the eternal youth principle, and declare that the truth of our being, the divinity of us, can not age, we shall not age prematurely in appearance. This habitual thought will outpicture itself on the body in harmony, in beauty and grace, instead of in wrinkles and other marks of old age.

We can not get away from the fact that it is impossible for us to be very different from our convictions. It is hard for a physician to keep a patient alive who believes he is going to die and that nothing can save him. The bodily conditions follow his faith.

I have known of several people who believed that they would not live beyond their sixtieth or sixty-fifth year and who had that point so definitely and firmly fixed in their conviction that as a matter of fact they did *not* live much beyond it. For years before their death this fixed period seemed to be the focal point of all their plans, thoughts, and acts.

Such false notions of longevity are very apt to prevail among those whose lives are bound hand and foot by a monotonous routine of existence.

In spite of fresh air, fresh fruits, vegetables, and the quiet, restful condition of rustic life, country people especially women, often age much faster than city people. This is generally due to the monotony of their lives, their lack of growth, of interest, of change. People whose minds run in a groove and who live the same kind of a life year in and year out, age rapidly. Their thoughts become ossified.

Mental ossification produces physical ossification. The hardening of the tissues, so indicative of advancing years, is invariably preceded by the hardening thought. The shriveling-up process, the wrinkles, all appear in the mind first.

Monotony is a rapid ager. Variety is characteristic of youth. The mind grows stale very quickly under a monotonous life, a humdrum existence.

A more hopeful outlook, greater immunity

from drudgery, — due to inventions and labor-saving devices, — more prosperity, saner, more optimistic philosophy, better sanitary conditions and more scientific living have all combined to prolong the average length of life many years. Already the life insurance tables recognize this fact.

Achievement of some kind seems essential to a long life. We were made to do things. Nothing, except dissipation, is so destructive of the youthful in man as idleness. "A man is not old while he is doing things, and if he is not doing anything he is dead."

Industry conduces to longevity. It is the ship at the wharf, not the ship at sea, that rots fastest; — the still pool, not the running brook, that stagnates. Honest, earnest endeavor tends to health of body and mind.

The unused faculties in our brain and other parts of the body age much more rapidly than those that are perpetually exercised. To retain our youth, we must keep alive all over.

To pile up insignificant years is not really living. When the years cease to count in growth, in enlargement, in usefulness, then we merely exist; we do not live. Some people walk about the earth a quarter of a century after they are practically dead, just as some trees stand for a long time after they have ceased to put forth leaves and the life has gone out of them.

It is not such a very difficult thing to freshen or rejuvenate the mind. It is just a question of holding the right thought vigorously, resolutely, perpetually. But it requires constant watching, perpetual endeavor, and invincible determination; just as it does to make a fortune or to achieve anything else worth while.

If you wish to appear young think of yourself as being constantly renewed, rejuvenated, for there is a perpetual renewal going on in the cells of your body. Think of youth as the everlasting fact and old age conditions as false, unnecessary, unnatural, caused largely by old age thought habits, race habits, old age convictions. Say to yourself, "I can not grow old because I am perpetually being made new, and new cells can not look old unless made so by old age thought and conviction."

Think life, live it; think youth, live it; feel it, express it from every pore of your being!

Persistently shut the doors to all the enemies of youth, all aging thoughts. Forget unpleasant experiences, disagreeable incidents. By harmonious thinking you may retain your youthfulness and increase your longevity enormously.

A happy domestic life has a great deal to do with prolonging existence. Friction of any kind, especially domestic friction, grinds life away at a fearful rate. There is only one way to maintain physical harmony, and that is to maintain mental harmony.

An English clergyman who lived to be one hundred and five years old, and who was often asked the secret of his longevity, replied, " I have made it a rule of my life never to think of anything disagreeable after nine o'clock at night."

Night worrying is not only painful and aging, but also dangerous. It keeps the blood in a state of chronic poisoning which impairs all of the mental processes and the physical functions as well.

The minds of many people have become unbalanced because they did not break the habit of night picturing, visualizing their troubles and trials, which are always so much exaggerated and appear in such fearful vividness during the night.

One of the great secrets of longevity is to learn how to retard the aging processes during sleep. Before falling into unconsciousness, we should fill the mind with bright, encouraging, inspiring thoughts. If our life vision has become dim or blackened during the trials of the day, we should clear it by erasing all the blackness and tearing down all the sable pictures, expelling all that is ugly and disagreeable, every thought which has made us unhappy or caused us to suffer.

We should never go to sleep until we have restored our lost balance, gained perfect mental poise, until we have put into operation the forces which would tend to harmonize and bring peace and joy into our lives.

Intelligence can do much to eliminate short life tendencies. Were man wise enough, he would be able to carry the freshness of youth into the teens of his second century.

One of the most hopeful signs of the times is the saner, more cheerful note in our religious life. There is not so much sadness in it. Many of the old, solemn, death-suggesting hymns have been dropped from our hymn books. When I was a boy people used to take a morbid delight in singing such dirges as, "Hark from the Tomb a Doleful Sound," "Death and Decay All Around Us," etc., which were once immensely popular, and which people then doubtless thought normal.

We enjoy more, laugh more, play more than did our ancestors. We are not so solemn or sad-faced, we do not take life in such a terribly serious way.

Men with trained minds often eliminate a great many of the weaknesses which prematurely cut off the ignorant and the untrained. Astronomers and other men whose minds deal with vast spaces and infinite periods of time tend to defy the physical weaknesses which help to shorten the lives of those who are occupied with harassing, vexing, material things.

The vocation has a great deal to do with longevity. Some callings cut away life at a fearful rate, — especially those in which people are obliged to work in close, dark factories or shops. The sunlight is a powerful rejuvenator and force producer. Darkness and shadows are death-dealing.

The simple life, — plain living and high thinking — tends to increase longevity. There is no doubt that because of the very nature of his work, the clergyman's life is conducive to longevity. His mind is employed on high themes; he contemplates sacred subjects. He is dealing with high ideals, and, for the most part, leads an unselfish life, largely devoted to the service of others.

A high ideal, a lofty purpose, a noble aim, whatever tends to make man look up and struggle up, tends to improve his health condition. The soul that aspires, other things being equal, has the longest life. Aspiration is a perpetual tonic; it stimulates all the faculties.

Our natures are framed upon principles of justice, honesty, truth, beauty; and, whenever we violate any of these principles in act or thought, there is discord within, and, of course, a corresponding waste of energy and vitality, and physical and mental deterioration.

We age rapidly because we do not keep our mental instruments in tune. Discord, grating and jarring whittle life away very quickly. We suffer when we are discordant because we have violated the fundamental law of divine harmony. Poise, mental serenity, is a friend of youth and tends to refresh, renew, and rejuvenate the body.

Many make the mistake of trying to keep young from without, by external application and manipulations, by covering up blemishes and defects and evidences of age.

I know a woman who for many years has had a horror of growing old. She is so afraid that people will see indications of her advancing years that she has become almost a mon-omaniac upon the subject. For some time she has worn a wig to conceal her white hair, and she is always in terror, especially when travel-ing, lest something will happen to reveal it. She uses all sorts of "make up" and devices for concealing her age.

If you would retain your youth, keep with the young as much as you can, because their exuberant spirits, their quick wits, bright minds, and youthful manners are infectious. Those who live much with the young are much more youthful than those who are much in the society of old people.

Look as though you were young. Dress as youthfully as is consistent with the dignity and good sense of your years. Do not stoop over, or shuffle your feet. Throw your shoul-ders back; walk erect, and youthfully; do not drag your steps.

Do not let romance die out of your heart. It is a great youth preserver. Love, unselfish-ness, a spirit of kindness and helpfulness, keep the heart warm and young.

Whenever you think of yourself, always hold the image of yourself *as you would like to be*. Do not dwell upon your imperfections or weaknesses, because that will mar your image, but hold tenaciously to the ideal of yourself; think of yourself in your perfection, as the personality the Creator intended you to be. Many people dwell in their thoughts upon their imperfections, and so accentuate their weaknesses or peculiarities that they only see a distorted picture of themselves. They gradually lose their self-respect and their dignity. It is what we think of ourselves, the ideal of ourselves which we have in mind, that out-pictures itself in our manner, our appearance.

It is very important to cultivate everything which will tend to keep the spirit fresh and young, the mind youthful and bright. Do not take life too seriously. If you do, you will not accomplish nearly as much, you will age faster, and will not be half as interesting nor have half as much fun as you otherwise would.

Lots of play and innocent fun tend to erase the marks of age and to bring us back to youth. Fun is a twin of youth. To be normally healthy we require a great deal of amusement and recreation and all of the innocent fun we can get, for these are great stimulators, life promoters.

A hard, critical, cold, over-serious mental attitude sours the mind by generating mental poisons, which accumulate in the system and make perfect health and happiness impossible. We often notice that over-serious, selfish, greedy characters age prematurely. Their skin soon wrinkles up. They have a hard, repellent expression; they are not magnetic or efficient.

Humor is a care-killer, a worry destroyer. It tends to quicken the circulation, to promote digestion. Cheerful people sleep better, are better company, and have more friends, and people who have many friends are less likely to be morose and depressed. Sociability is a promoter of good will, kindly feelings, and harmony; and all these things induce health and prolong life.

Other things being equal, it is the merry heart that lives longest.

Growth is an enemy of old age. The man who is mentally expanding, who is constantly growing larger and becoming broader, fuller, completer, does not age nearly as rapidly as the man who has ceased to grow.

Age begins when growth stops. When the mind ceases to expand, to reach out and up, when the ideals begin to grow dim, when aspiration halts, then old age steps in.

Dry rot, inaction, are great enemies of youthful conditions. To be perpetually alive on all sides of one's nature is the price of retaining

one's youth. If you are anxious to avoid
growing old prematurely, keep your mind
active, buttressed with new ideas. Be abreast
of the times, interested in the world's progress.
While a person is fresh and interesting we do
not count his years.

What is more delightful and inspiring
than an old man full of hope, who is optimistic, cheerful, boyish in his humor, earnest
in his purpose, enthusiastic in his work — a
man who has grown kinder as he has grown
older; who has not soured on life, has never
lost his faith in his fellow men; who has a
grace of personality which comes from a sweetness of temper and a fine and delicate nature?

The man who feels the spirit of youth surg-
ing through his body all the time, who holds
the bright, cheerful, youthful, hopeful thought,
retains his youthful appearance.

Swedenborg taught that the aged are constantly advancing toward the springtime of
their youth, so that those who have lived longest are really the youngest.

*The time will come when age will be
marked only by a mightier momentum,* and
the more years a man has lived, the more he
will be revered, admired, and sought after,
not through a sense of pity, because he is

weak and dependent, but because he is *a mightier man.*

Old age ought to be extremely attractive, powerful, and beautiful. The coming man — the possible man — will so grow old that every year will merely be so much addition in growth and development to what he was the year before. His whole life will be cumulative in wisdom and power.

" Age is not all decay," says George McDonald, " it is the ripening and swelling of the fresh life within that withers and bursts the husks."

There is a vast difference between ripening and blighting. A perfectly normal old age is beautiful, serene, and lovely; is an enriching, sweetening process, — a process which brings out qualities far more luscious than are found in the green fruit of earlier life.

There are a multitude of reasons why the last of life should be the best of life.

When we learn the great truth that no power can separate us from the God principle, that our life and health and immortality are in the God (good) within us, we shall be able to resist the ravages of time and to realize that there is no dissolution of the *reality* of us in what we call death.

XIV. AS A MAN THINKETH

XIV. AS A MAN THINKETH

> We scatter seeds with a careless hand
> And dream we ne'er shall see them more;
>   But for a thousand years
>   Their fruit appears,
> In weeds that mar the land. —JOHN KEBLE.

> You never can tell what your thoughts will do
>   In bringing you hate or love,
> For thoughts are things, and their airy wings
>   Are swift as a carrier dove.
> They follow the law of the universe—
>   Each thing must create its kind—
> And they speed o'er the track to bring you back,
>   Whatever went out from your mind.
>   —ELLA WHEELER WILCOX.

"When we once realize that by driving away pessimistic, angry and bitter thoughts we drive away sickness and misfortune to a great extent, and that by seeking the kinder and happier frame of mind we seek at the same time success and health and good luck, we will find a new impetus in the control of our mental forces."

 Y analyzing the light of a star, although millions of miles away, we can tell what metals are burning in its incandescent atmosphere. Each metal casts a bar across the spectrum, when the light is passed through a prism, which is characteristic of its own quality.

An experienced mental chemist could analyze a person's character, even if a stranger, and tell what discordant thought or vicious ideal is casting its fatal shadow upon his personality.

Things have just the power over us with which we endow them. That which strikes terror to one person's heart and paralyzes his efficiency may not cause another even to wince. I know a few persons who have so trained their thought that they allow nothing to shake them from their center.

One, for example, has lost all his property, all his family, and he is left alone in the world a poor and homeless old man. Yet no one can ever detect a tremor of complaint or a weakness anywhere in his nature, simply because he has so completely learned the science of right thinking that he can shut out of his mind or neutralize with its mental antidote anything which would cause him pain or injury. He neutralizes discord with harmony, error with truth.

He has become such an adept at mental chemistry that the very moment he is touched with the poison of hatred and jealousy, he antidotes it with love, the spirit of good-will. The shafts of malice and envy can not get near him. He looks upon these things as no part of the truth of his being.

When you are suffering from fear or worry, you may be sure you have endowed something with this power over you, otherwise it could not have gained such a hold. The very fact that you fear it shows that you have established between it and yourself a relation which you could break if you only knew how to apply your mental chemistry. Whenever you are unhappy, distressed, "blue," worried, it is due to some mental poison, which ought to be as easy to antidote as it is to destroy fire with water.

We are just beginning to see the wonderful scientific truth in the philosophy which tells us to love our enemies, because if we hate them we merely add more fuel to passion's fire, while love puts it out. The love thought neutralizes hatred, jealousy, and makes friends of our enemies. There is nothing in love which can make an enemy. The injunction to love our enemies is, therefore, as scientific as the advice to put out fire by water.

How quickly and effectively the purity thought destroys and neutralizes the impure thought, the sensual suggestion! Who has not seen the marvelous transformation which pure, unselfish love has wrought in a foul, beastly nature in a comparatively short time?

The things that come from others correspond with what we send to them. What we are trying to see in them we find there. If we are trying to see good, to find what is noble, clean, and true, their affinities spring out to meet our own. But if, on the other hand, we look for the bad, we are likely to find it. If we have a mean, jealous, envious, contemptible thought towards others, if we are looking for the brute in them, the brute will come out to meet us. We radiate to others our own estimate of them, our own thought of them. Every person we meet gives us a little different estimate of ourselves.

What you allow to live in your heart, harbor in your mind, dwell upon in your thoughts, are seeds which will develop in your life and produce things like themselves. Hate seed in the heart can not produce a love flower in the life. A sinister thought will produce a sinister harvest. The revenge seed will produce a bloody harvest.

Whatever goes from you to others calls out from them the same kind of qualities to meet your own. If the God within you — the ineffable spirit of love, of charity — speaks to a man, although he may be a criminal, the God will come out of him to meet it; but if you fling out diabolical, satanic forces, — hatred, jealousy, envy, — they will arouse and call out the devil from the victim of your thought radiation. Good will come out to meet good, evil in response to evil; hatred comes out to meet hatred, love to meet love, because they are affinities. Thought obeys a law as inexorable as that of mathematics. No love can return in exchange for a hatred thought; but if your thought is freighted with love, love will come back to meet its own. To have friends we must show ourselves friendly. To be loved, we must love.

Even the brute natures respond to the quality of our thought. An animal tamer can lead a wild beast with a string by the use of kindness and gentleness, when ten men by only using force might not be able to make it move. There is something within us which leaps forth to meet kindness and gentleness, and there is also something of the brute within us which leaps forth to meet the brute impulse.

"If a man purposely does me wrong," a Buddhist says, "I will return him my ungrudging love; the more evil comes from him, the more good shall go from me."

The time will come when one will no more allow discordant thoughts in his mind than he would scatter thistle seeds over his garden.

Everybody who sees your present character, your moral harvest, knows what you put into the soil of your youth. They do not need to go back and inquire about your childhood; the crop tells the story; you are simply reaping what you have sown. You do not expect to get the fragrant breath of the rose from sowing thistle seeds. How can you expect to sow the thistles of revenge and brutality and reap a harvest of kindness and happiness?

On the other hand, if we sow the charitable, magnanimous, encouraging, uplifting thought, we shall reap the golden harvest of harmony and beauty and joy. If we sow the thoughts of abundance, of plenty, we shall tend to reap prosperity; while if we sow the mean, pinched, stingy failure thoughts, we shall reap a poverty harvest.

When we see a sour, repulsive face, we know that it is a harvest of selfish, vicious sowing. And when we see a serene, confident face, we know that it has come from the sowing of harmonious, helpful, unselfish thought seeds.

Many people seem to think that we are huddled together in a world of chance, buffeted about by a cruel destiny; but the fact is that we are in a current which runs Heavenward in a world of absolute law and order, where nothing happens by chance — nothing without a cause, a *sufficient* cause, — where the minutest detail of our lives obeys a law as unerring as that which holds the heavenly bodies in their courses with such perfect adjustment that they do not vary a fraction of a second in a century in their orbits of untold millions of miles.

Wherever we see discord, we know that it is a harvest from discordant sowing. Nothing else is possible. Discord of every kind, whether it is expressed in suffering, in disease, in poverty, in failure, in happiness, simply means that one is out of harmony with his better self, that he does not harmonize with his divinity.

The man who is always complaining of his lot and whining and blaming other people for his misfortunes is not a real man. He is only an apology of the man God intended him to be. Sometime, somewhere, we shall learn to protect ourselves from our thought enemies, killing emotion enemies, just as we protect our homes from thieves. We shall learn to shut out from the mind, or antidote with their opposites all discordant thoughts, because of the dread of the pain and suffering, the humiliation, the mortification they cause us, and the fatal harvest they produce.

Is there anything more scientific, when the body is the product of the mind, than that a morbid mind filled with sick thoughts should produce a morbid, sick body? Can we expect the functions to act normally when the thoughts, the body builders, are abnormal?

Physical discord always means mental discord, for if there had always been perfect harmony in the mind, the body would be in harmony. So, if you can keep the mind in perfect harmony, the body must ultimately correspond, because the physical is merely an outpicturing of the mental.

We shall some time learn that only the good is true; that harmony is the reality; that discord is merely the absence of it. There is only one Creator, and He made all that is made; hence everything must be in His likeness, perfect; nothing that is real can be unlike Him, and, therefore, only the good, the harmonious, the pure, the clean, the true *can* be real. All else must be false, a seeming, a delusion. God could not create anything unlike himself.

God is principle and principle can not change. Whatever is wrong in the world can not come from Him, from perfection, from right, from good, and must therefore be accounted for in some other way.

Savages and primitive peoples have great faith in the fact that the Creator put into certain barks, plants, and minerals remedies for every physical ill. But we are beginning to learn that man carries the *great* panacea for all his ills within himself; that the antidotes for the worst poisons, the poisons of hatred, jealousy, anger, and selfishness, exist in the form of love, charity, and good-will essences, in his own mind.

The cheerful, hopeful thought is itself a powerful remedy for a score of ills, such as the " blues," melancholia, and discouragement. Optimism alone is an antidote for some of the worst mental diseases.

Hold to optimistic ideals, and you will drive out pessimism, the great breeder of disease, failure, and misery. Stand guard at the door of your mind; keep out all the enemies of your happiness and achievement, and you will be astonished at your increased power and entire change of life within a short time.

The habit of holding the thought of health,

the thought of strength, vigor, and robustness as a present reality, as an everlasting fact, is a wonderful tonic and will soon give a consciousness of increasing power. We shall feel that we are being buttressed and supported by almighty Principle, because our thoughts and sentiments are surcharged with life and truth, and are creative.

All thoughts which suggest weakness, failure, unhappiness, or poverty, are destructive, negative, tearing-down thoughts. They are our enemies. Brand them whenever they try to gain an entrance into your mind. Avoid them as you would thieves, for they *are* thieves, thieves of our comfort, thieves of harmony, of power, of happiness, of success.

Every true, beautiful, and helpful thought is a suggestion which, if held in the mind, tends to reproduce itself there — clarifies the ideals and uplifts the life. While these inspiring and helpful suggestions fill the mind their opposites can not get in their deadly work, because the two can not possibly live together. They are natural enemies.

We tend to grow more and more like that which we cherish, harbor, and constantly long for, and to lose or become unlike that which we hate, despise, and habitually deny. The latter gradually loses its grip upon our lives, releases its hold upon character, and finally vanishes.

The persistent denial of the theory that we are poor, miserable worms of the dust, victims of limitation, of weakness, tending towards depravity, and the stout affirmation of the dominance of truth and beauty will bring out marvelous beauties of character. That which is constantly and persistently denied will ultimately fade out of the consciousness and go out of the life.

A tremendous power permeates the life and solidifies the character from holding perpetually the life-thought, the truth-thought, the optimistic thought, and the beauty-thought. The one who has the secret takes hold of the very fundamental principles of the universe, gets down to the verity of things, and lives in reality itself. A sense of security, of power, of calmness and repose comes to those who are conscious of being enveloped in the very center of truth and reality which can never come to those who live on the surface of things.

It is impossible to estimate the value of the quality of our everyday habits of thought. It makes all the difference in the world whether these habits are healthful or morbid, and

whether they lead to soundness or to rotten-
ness. The quality of the thought fixes the
quality of the ideal. The ideal can not be
high if the thought is low. It is worth everything to face life with the right outlook, — a
healthful, cheerful, optimistic outlook, — with
hope that has sunshine in it. People who radiate successful, joyful, helpful thoughts, who
scatter sunshine wherever they go, are the
helpers of the world, the lighteners of bur-
dens, who ease the jolts of life, soothe the
wounded, and give solace to the discouraged.

Learn to radiate joy, not stingily, not
meanly, but generously. Fling out your gladness without reserve. Shed it in the home,
on the street, on the car, in the store, everywhere, as the rose sheds its beauty and gives
out its fragrance. When we learn that love
thoughts heal, that they carry balm to wounds;
that thoughts of harmony, of beauty, and of
truth always uplift and ennoble; that the opposite carry death and destruction and blight
everywhere, we shall know the secret of right
living.

Some people harbor for years a bitter hatred
or a great jealousy toward others. Although
he may not be aware of it, such a mental attitude unfits the possessor for expressing the

maximum of his ability, and destroys his happiness. And not only this; but he radiates his inimical atmosphere, thus prejudicing people against him, arousing antagonism, and constantly handicapping himself all along the line.

The mind must be kept free from bitterness, jealousy, hatred, envy, and uncharitable thoughts; free from everything which trammels it, or there must be a penalty paid in impaired efficiency and inferior work as well as loss of peace of mind.

No one can do his best work while he harbors revengeful or even unfriendly thoughts toward others. Our faculties only give up their best when working in perfect harmony. There must be good-will in the heart or we can not do good work with head or hand.

Hatred, revenge, and jealousy are rank poisons, as fatal to all that is noblest in us as arsenic is fatal to the physical life.

A kindly attitude, a feeling of good will toward others, is our best protection against bitter hatred or injurious thoughts of any kind, for they can not penetrate the love shield, the good-will shield.

How easily, beautifully, and sweetly some people go through life, with very little to jar them or to disturb their equanimity! They have no discord in their lives because their natures are harmonious. They seem to love everybody, and everybody loves them. They have no enemies, because they do not arouse antagonism, hence they have little suffering or trouble.

Others, with ugly, crabbed, cross-grained dispositions, are always in hot water. They are always misunderstood; people are constantly hurting them. They generate discord because they are discordant themselves.

No one can carry secret hatreds and grudges, jealousies, and revengeful feelings, without seriously impairing his own reputation. Many people wonder why they are not popular, why they are disliked generally, why they stand for so little in their community, when it is really because of their bitter, revengeful, discordant radiations which kill personal magnetism.

On the other hand, those who send out kindly, loving, helpful, sympathetic thoughts, those who feel friendly toward everybody, and who carry no bitterness, hatred, or jealousy in their hearts, are attractive, helpful, and sunny.

The coming man will realize that every discordant thought, every effort to take an unfair advantage of another, to get that which does not justly belong to him, will cause him injury out of all proportion to the benefit received. He will find that things are so arranged in this world that no departure from justice, equity, honesty, and unselfishness is worth while. The time will come when every human being will want to do right and be just and true if only because it will bring joy and peace and prosperity.

Man will reach the millennium when he has learned to hold the right attitude of mind towards his fellow men. The time will come when it will be found infinitely easier to do right than to do wrong, when people will eagerly follow the Golden Rule, because it will produce harmony and universal well-being.

XV. MENTAL SELF-THOUGHT POISONING

XV. MENTAL SELF-THOUGHT POI-SONING

Every thought or emotion vibrates through every cell in the body and leaves an influence like itself.

The coming man will find it as easy to counteract an unfriendly, disagreeable thought, by turning on the counter-thought which will antidote or neutralize it, as it is to rob the hot water of its burning power by turning on the cold water faucet.

The hatred thought can not live an instant in the presence of the love thought.

"He who hates is an assassin"—and he is also a suicide.

"Right thinking pays large dividends."

NE of the most unfortunate convictions that ever entered the human brain is the idea which multitudes of people have that, on account of the weaknesses and disease tendencies inherited from those who have broken health laws for centuries back of them, they are not supposed to have a perfect body or good health. It is a wonder that the bodily organs and functions work as well as they do and that there is any

such thing as real health with such a cramping, crippling thought; for the body is but a mass of billions of cells so closely tied together and interrelated that they are instantly affected by every vicious thought, mood, or unfortunate conviction.

The normal law of our lives is wholeness. Discord of any kind — ill health, disease, weakness — is abnormal, foreign to our real selves, to the truth of our being.

New thought builds new cells, life cells, youth cells in the body, just as the old style of thinking, the worry thought, the aging thought, the discordant thought, builds cells which correspond. The time will come when we shall listen to the cry of the cells suffering from disease and discord, just as we now listen to the cry of a child, and shall antidote the discord with the soothing, healing thought balm. We shall speak harmony, peace, health to the discordant cells until the disease is neutralized and harmony reigns.

Multitudes of people are in worse bondage to-day than were the African slaves before the war. Their masters are such things as a draught of cold air, wet feet, anything that is "fried," all sorts of superstitions, which they fear as much as the slave ever feared his master.

If such people want to go on a journey, to write a book, to plead a case at the bar, to sing, to paint, they must first consult their body, and if it says "no" they quit. If it says it is tired or weary or sick, no matter what duty or the great life purpose may say, they must wait until the body is good and ready.

But the time will come when we shall be ashamed to refer to our ailments, our physical weaknesses, because it will be regarded as an evidence that, at least in thought, we have sinned; an evidence that we have been holding unkind, unjust, vicious thoughts towards others, thoughts of revenge or hatred, a desire to "get square" for some fancied injury; an evidence that we have been selfish, jealous, or that we have been dishonest, have been taking unfair advantage of others in some way, or that through fear or worry or some other form of mental discord, we have been the victims of self-thought poisoning.

It will be considered evidence that we are not living properly, that we are breaking some of nature's laws, or that our ancestors have done so: evidence that our body has been poisoned by vicious or impure thoughts, that we have in some way lost control of ourselves.

To be healthy, happy, and successful we

must be good. There is no other road to true happiness and real prosperity.

In the phonograph records of some of our great singers, the slightest error — a note a little too sharp or flat — is faithfully reproduced. In just the same way every mistake, every sidestep from virtue, every slip, every blunder we make in life is faithfully recorded in our cell phonograph. The phonograph will only say the words that are on the record. You will have to make a record which has on it the words, the sentiment, you want the machine to repeat.

Your poor health to-day is but the expression of bad or vicious-living phonograph records recorded in your mind somewhere in the past, or in those who have gone before you. These records are scientifically accurate, and, once made, they are certain to be faithfully reproduced.

Few people realize that they are constantly running thoughts through their minds and indulging in emotions and passions which are disease producers. Every evil feeling towards another is a little disease producer. Every discordant thought, feeling, or emotion must pay the penalty in the physical manifestation of some discord.

When we are sufficiently tired of expressing disease and physical discords generally, we shall be careful only to record that which we wish to express — harmony, health, truth, and beauty.

Since we know that whatever we hold in the mental attitude will be reproduced in the body, how comparatively easy and scientific character-building and man-building should become! This is especially true, as we know that even thoughts, ideals, sentiments, and emotions which are only mechanically assumed are still the pattern for reproduction and become faithfully outpictured in the life.

Whatever we think about a great deal, we tend to become like. If we keep the mind concentrated much upon divine things, upon spiritual qualities, we not only tend to become spiritually-minded, but the quality also is out-pictured in our face and manner. How easily we can pick out of a crowd, the clergyman, or one in whom the dominant thought has dwelt long upon sacred things! By the constant picturing of divine qualities, holy things, wholeness, completeness, perfection of character, they become outpictured in the features, look out of the eyes, or speak through the face and manner. In the same way we

can tell the physician, the lawyer, the clerk.
The dominant thought, whatever has been
uppermost in their minds, whatever their
minds have been habitually long concentrated
upon, becomes outpictured in the face, manner,
and conversation, so that we can read the signs
and ear-marks.

Did you ever realize that it is possible to
read in your face and manner the record of
your thoughts; that your face is a bulletin
board upon which is advertised what has been
going on in your mind for years?

It was a saying of Swedenborg that "a man
writes his life in his physique; and thus the
angels discover his autobiography in his
structure."

There is a picture of your greed, revenge,
selfishness, jealousy — a record of your dominant passion, which the world can read. You
may have supposed that your thoughts were
secret; but the fact is that they are all dis-
played upon your face bulletin.

In reality, we can hide nothing, for we
radiate the truth of ourselves. What we
think is written on the countenance. Our faces
are covered with the scars, the wounds, which
our boomerang thoughts have made, for every
vicious thought is a boomerang. If we throw

a jealous or an envious or revengeful thought to another, it by an inexorable law comes back and wounds the thrower.

It is just as possible to establish health on a solid, substantial, permanent basis as it is to establish a business. *Right thinking and right living make a right life.* The body, being a product of the mind, must necessarily be like it.

If we think truth and harmony, if we carry the beauty thought, the love thought, these principles will be outpictured in the body. A discordant body can not come from harmonious thinking.

It is well known that inflammation or trouble of any kind anywhere in the body is aggravated by concentrating the mind upon it or worrying about it.

The only way to attain perfect health is to grow into the complete realization of more health, greater vigor. We can not be physically vigorous until we hold the vigorous thought.

Many people make robust health impossible by holding the sickly thought, the thought of their weakness, the picture of diseased tissues somewhere in the body, and, of course, their general health corresponds with this diseased model, for the thought furnishes the pattern which is reproduced in the body.

Always try to realize that truth, health, and harmony are not something far away from you, but are always with you, *in you.* Realizing their presence as an actual present fact will help you wonderfully.

A healthy body is composed of healthy thought externalized, outpictured. And, too, it follows the ideals, and as long as one holds the youthful, vigorous, progressive, energetic, creative ideal in his mind his body responds to the thought.

Just try the experiment of thinking of yourself as an absolutely perfect being, possessing superb health, a magnificent body, a vigorous constitution, a sublime mind, and capable of standing any amount of strain.

Never allow yourself to have a defective, crippled, dwarfed ideal of yourself; never entertain such an imperfect health model for an instant, for these mental patterns of yourself will gradually begin to be reproduced in your physical condition.

Your ideal, your conviction of your health, is the pattern which the life processes are constantly weaving into your body.

Our ideas, ideals, thoughts, emotions, moods,

our mental attitude, send a constant succession of vibrations through every cell, every organ, and through all the functions of the body. There is a perpetual succession of these impulses through the entire mass of the millions of cells.

If we scratch with a nail or some other hard substance on the end of a long piece of timber, the sound waves are transferred through the entire length. Every cell in the huge timber feels the vibration and passes it on. So, every thought, emotion, every sense of fear, worry, jealousy, hatred, that enters the mind instantly makes itself felt through every cell in the body, and affects it according to its own nature.

A happy, joyous, uplifting thought or emotion sends its message of life and healing like lightning to the remotest cells in the body.

On the other hand, every discordant emotion, every thought of hatred, jealousy, or selfishness sends its poisonous contagion through every one of the billions of cells.

It is now well established that vicious mental states, violent emotions and explosive passions, make chemical changes in the brain and poison the cell life through the whole body.

We are beginning to learn that the cells of the stomach and of all the other organs are but an extended brain, so to speak, and that they are very seriously affected by anything which affects the brain. Hence all the bodily functions refuse to do good work when the mind is disturbed, just as the mental faculties refuse to give up their best when they are in discord.

It is very unfortunate that there is such a deep-seated conviction in the human race that the mind is *confined* to the brain cells alone. There is every evidence that there is intelligence in cells all through the body. This theory has been corroborated and substantiated by the fact that very large portions of the brain have been removed from an individual without very materially impairing his intelligence.

Many interesting experiments have been made to prove this theory. If we slice a bit of tissue, which, of course, is all cells, from any part of the living body and put it upon a slide of the microscope where there is the least trace of nitro-glycerin, the cells quickly, instinctively, shrink from contact with the powerful chemical, drawing themselves back as far as possible from the poisonous substance, which they evidently regard as their fatal enemy.

On the other hand, if we bring it in contact with some harmless drug such as capsicum, instead of shrinking they rush towards it and give every evidence that they like it.

If we put opium in contact with these cells they vibrate rapidly as though in a fatal tremor, and quickly succumb to its influence and become narcotized.

We find this power of selection even in the lowest forms of animal life, such as the amœba, the simplest form of one-cell structure. Even where there is no brain structure whatever the cell recognizes its enemies, from which it tries to make escape and to seek a hiding-place.

The whole body is a mass of cells, and this is why the cells in any part of the body, when disarranged or diseased, respond so quickly to mental treatment. It is because there is intelligence in them, because they are a part of the mind themselves. They have a mental quality, and the combined mentality of the brain cells and all the other cells in the body can restore any group of cells in any organ or tissue when they begin to shrink and shrivel, as in old age, or when they become diseased.

Mind is the great healer, the great restorer, because it was the original creator of these cells. It is the *mind* within and back of the cell structure that responds to mental treatment, restores the lost balance, and heals the disease.

Body and mind are one. Untold harm has come to the race through the belief that they are distinct. All the intelligence that is in us is distributed through the cells of the body. These cells are all specialists and all more or less intelligent, and the combined intelligence of all of the cells of the entire body forms the intelligence of the individual. It may be true that there is a higher development of intelligence in the brain cells, but there is a wonderful help in regarding your whole body as a brain, as being permeated with Divine intelligence, because every cell is in the closest touch with the Divine force, which creates, sustains, heals, restores, and renews. And when we become conscious that every cell in our body is a Divine thing, where all health and harmony and beauty and truth and love reside, we shall then know what it is to taste power.

The different organs are especially susceptible to certain kinds of mental influence.

Excessive selfishness and envy seriously affect the liver, while the heart, liver, and spleen are strongly influenced by jealousy, especially when chronic.

It is well known that violent, long-continued jealousy affects the heart's action most injuriously, as do all sorts of mental discord, such as worry, anxiety, fear, anger, especially where they become chronic. One night of mental agony has often caused the well to become invalids. Constant grief, long-standing and bitter jealousy, perpetual care and corroding anxiety, tend to develop disease.

I know a man who so poisons his system in a few minutes by a hot temper that he does not get over it for days. Jealousy will so poison the system as completely to change the nature of its victim in a very short time. There is nothing which will burn out the life cells and ruin harmony and efficiency quicker than the violent indulgence of the explosive passions. Indigestion or dyspepsia often follow fierce domestic quarrels. Multitudes of people have died from heart trouble induced by uncontrolled passions.

Intense hatred, violent fits of anger, and some forms of worry have a very irritating and poisoning influence upon the kidneys and materially aggravate certain forms of kidney disease. Jaundice often follows great mental shocks and violent outbursts of hot temper. People are frequently made bilious by despondency, fear, and worry, which, in fact, are deadly enemies of the kidneys and the skin, and seriously prevent the elimination of poisons.

These structural changes in the different organs are due to chemical changes in the development through mental influence of poisonous substances in the tissues.

Whenever there is any disturbance in the mind from any cause there is starvation in the tissues of the body, because perfect nourishment for the functions is impossible when discord is present anywhere.

The digestive organs — the liver and stomach for instance — are so dependent upon harmony that when there is the slightest mental disturbance they can not act normally, and digestion is interfered with.

It does not follow because you eat a great deal that you are properly nourished. It often happens that owing to the impairment of the efficiency of the digestive fluids, or through mental poisoning from mental discord, many of the tissues, even when there is plenty of food in the digestive organs, suffer seriously from starvation.

During fits of anger and jealousy, acute worry, or when one is suffering from fear, the gastric juices, for example, are very deficient in digestive essentials, become much diluted, and hence can only partially digest the food. They are entirely lacking in some of the ingredients which are absolutely necessary to perfect digestion and assimilation.

While it is true that chemical changes in the system which generate poison are often caused by overeating, irregular eating, and eating incompatible things which should never be taken into the stomach at the same time, yet many can be traced to mental causes, and are often chronic from the continued presence of such poison, as in the case of an habitual worrier.

In the first place, when gastric juice is secreted under unfavorable conditions, during mental depression, when the person is suffering from fear, worry, jealousy, revenge, anger, or hatred, it is of a very inferior quality. There is something lacking; it is not a perfect digestive fluid. The chemical proportions are not normal, and, in fact, there is often actual poison present.

Some people so poison themselves mentally during their meals that they can not digest their food. It is a dangerous thing to quarrel and to be angry and hateful at any time, but especially so during meals. Whatever you do, do not take your troubles to the table with you, for there is nothing which will ruin digestion quicker than a troubled, worried mind.

However uncomfortable, unhappy, worried, or troubled you may be at other times of the day, it is absolutely imperative to keep as happy and as harmonious as possible during meals and the digestive hours; otherwise the gastric fluids will seriously lack the essential digestive element.

People who carry their crotchets and worries to the table and who bring their surly, ugly moods to their meals poison everything they eat.

This is one reason why chronic worriers, people who are constant sufferers from fear and anxiety and the effects of their explosive passions, are often semi-invalids. Chronic worriers are never good digestors.

It is worth your while to make a determined effort to form the habit of good cheer during meals and before going to sleep, because it will have a powerful influence upon your health.

We all know how quickly our digestion is affected by our moods, our mental processes, our mental attitude. A sudden shock caused by a telegram or letter containing bad news will often completely arrest the entire digestive processes, which will not be resumed until the mind is again in comparative harmony.

If we could examine the stomach after a severe mental shock from bad news, we should find the natural flow of digestive fluids from the digestive follicles suspended; the follicles would be parched and feverish and for the time absolutely deprived of their digestive power.

So closely is the digestive apparatus connected with the brain that an accident of any kind, or great fear, will instantly stop all of its processes, just as though they had received an imperative command to cease working.

Discordant thought, fits of anger, jealousy, despondency, unpleasant sensations of every kind, seriously affect the digestion.

The finding of disgusting things mingled with our food will often so affect our stomachs that we can not eat anything for some time afterwards. Our sensation of hunger departs instantly and the very thought of food nauseates us. Just think of the tremendous power thought must have to cause this instantaneous revulsion and complete cessation of all the digestive processes!

Since physicians the world over now admit that dyspepsia, like many other ills, is a mental

disease, it is clear that if you persist in holding
the cheerful, harmonious, healthful thought,
instead of the despondent, inharmonious, un-
healthful thought, which upsets and demor-
alizes digestion, you will be able to overcome it,
as well as many other physical ills that result
from wrong thought.

The digestive processes follow the mental
processes, and coincide with them. If we
persistently, habitually, hold joy thoughts, contentment thoughts, good-will thoughts, which
are always working in us for health, and which
produce harmony, serenity, and poise, we tend
to establish mental health, and when this is
done, the body will fall into line. On the other
hand, discordant, inharmonious thoughts will
manifest themselves in various forms in the
body, now rheumatism, now dyspepsia, head-
ache or some other form of ill health.

The circulation of the blood is also very
seriously affected by all thoughts which depress
and discourage.

Many people, after prolonged fits of anger
or acute attacks of jealousy and fear, have
colds, indigestion, bilious attacks, sick or
nervous headaches.

Some have perpetual severe headaches, which
are due to mental poisoning from violent fits

of anger and the resultant general shock to the mental system, and also to impairment of nerve nutrition. Many suffer from perpetual selfishness-poisoning.

Poisons are generated in the brain cells by the chemical changes of the various thoughts, emotions, and explosive passions, no physical force being brought into play. When a black, discouraged thought-wave sweeps through the system, there comes with it a sense of depression, almost of terror. A single fit of hot temper may sometimes burn out the nerve centers, just as a short circuit will burn out the electric wires.

It is pitiful to see the wreckage of hopes, happiness, and ambition in a life after hurricanes of passion have swept through the mental kingdom.

Why do we learn so quickly that on the physical plane hot things burn us, sharp tools cut us, bruises make us suffer, and endeavor to avoid the things which give pain, and to use and enjoy the things that give pleasure and comfort; while in the mental realm we are constantly burning ourselves, gashing ourselves, poisoning our brain, our blood, our secretions with deadly, destructive thoughts, moods, and emotions? How we suffer from these thought lacerations, these mental bruises, these burnings of passion; and yet we do not learn to exclude the causes of all this suffering!

We are much more susceptible to disease when suffering from any sort of mental discord, discouragement, or the "blues," because of the cell damage due to the presence of chemical changes, the impairment of nutrition, imperfect digestion, and mental self-poisoning.

When discordant from worry, anxiety, anger, revenge, or jealousy, you may know that these things drain away your energy, waste your vitality at a fearful rate, and not only do no good, but also grind away the delicate mental machinery, inducing premature age and shortening the life. Worry thoughts, fear thoughts, selfish thoughts are so many malignant forces within us, destroying harmony and ruining efficiency, while the opposite thoughts produce just the opposite result. They soothe instead of irritate, and increase efficiency, multiply mental power. Five minutes of hot temper may work such a havoc in the delicate cell life of the nervous system that it will take weeks or months to repair the injury, or it may never be repaired.

Many people keep themselves in a state of chronic self-poisoning by their embittered, revengeful, hatred, jealous thoughts, selfishness, or by their violent tempers and fits of raging passion. These self-poisoners not only destroy their present happiness and success, but also many years of their lives.

When we fully realize, that these emotions and all forms of animal passion are debilitating, demoralizing, that they make fearful havoc in the mental realm, and that their hideousness is outpictured in the body in pain and suffering, in corresponding ugliness and deformities, we shall learn to avoid them as we would avoid physical pestilence.

There are authentic cases in our medical records of chronic invalids who have been completely cured by some sudden good news of relatives or friends whom they mourned as dead and who were found to be alive, or of some fortune which was suddenly and unexpectedly left them while they were very poor. These changes were produced by changing the thought.

It is well known that men are often severely wounded in battle by shot or shell, yet during the excitement they are totally unconscious of pain or of any serious injury to themselves, until, perhaps, they discover their blood-soaked clothing, or some one tells them that they are shot. Then, as soon as the excitement abates, the very consciousness of their condition, with the power of the imagination to exaggerate, causes them to collapse. But, while the mind was intensely occupied, they did not feel the bullet or the piece of shell.

We have all felt severe pain entirely cease during moments of great joy, when some unexpected good luck has come to us. The mind, for the time at least, was able to dominate the body and conquer pain.

I have known hunters completely exhausted by a day's tramp, perhaps in rain or snow without any results, and scarcely able to put one foot ahead of the other, who became instantly so transformed at the sight of the long-looked-for deer or moose that they forgot their hunger, their fatigue, and were as lively as boys. The change of mental attitude enabled them to tramp again for hours without rest and yet without fatigue.

Whatever improves the health of the mind improves the health of the body. The uplifting, inspiring, cheerful and optimistic thought is not only a great mental tonic, but a physical tonic also.

How can your body have resisting power to ward off disease when you are all the time acknowledging its weakness and inferiority? How can you expect harmony in your physical kingdom when you are constantly reflecting mental discord?

Never allow yourself to be convinced that you are not complete master of yourself. Stoutly affirm your own superiority over bodily ills, and do not acknowledge yourself the slave of an inferior power.

Nothing else will hasten the development of a disease so quickly as that attitude of mind which tends to lower the vitality by constantly looking for the thing we dread, always expecting and watching for every symptom which heralds it, because we are powerfully affected by the imagination, which builds all sorts of hideous predictions and forebodings out of the things we fear and dread.

This perpetual expectancy of something which is going to make us suffer and finally kill us has a terribly depressing influence, because it cuts off hope and expectancy — the very things we live upon. It dries up the very source of life and vitality, and causes the victim to fail rapidly.

Think of the influence upon a sensitive nature of carrying for years the conviction that he has inherited a terrible malady, that he has lurking in his system an incipient disease that will ultimately kill him! All of his secretions are very materially influenced and the quality of the blood is deteriorated by such a conviction, for it is well known that worry, anxiety, fear, kill millions and millions of red-blood corpuscles every day.

When a physician is tactless enough to tell his patient of his critical condition, there is an immediate sinking, often a fatal collapse, so rapidly do the red-blood globules die under a fatal dread and apprehension. There is no doubt that thousands of patients have been killed by the brutal plainness of physicians, when under cheerful, hopeful encouragement they might have recovered. Hope and cheer are infinitely better tonics than any drugs. In fact, there is little danger as long as the courage and cheerfulness of the patient can be maintained, for the reactive influence upon all the functions of the body is very powerful.

Every physician knows what a tremendous healing, restorative force comes to a patient who has been in great danger when he is assured by a physician in whom he has great confidence that he is going to get well. The mere expectancy of relief from suffering through some noted specialist or a remedy in

which he has great faith often materially affects
the chemistry of the patient's body in all its
physical processes, arouses the healing potencies, creative energies within him, and
completely changes him.

In fact, his whole outlook upon life is often
changed by this new-born hope, this uplifting
expectancy, which the long-looked-for precious
remedy or celebrated physician brings, and the
patient begins to feel better even before the
prescription has been filled.

There is often a very marked improvement
in the patient immediately after taking the
medicine in which he implicitly believes, even
before it could possibly have been absorbed and
assimilated in the system, showing conclusively
that the expectancy, the faith, alone, did the
work.

It is expectancy, implicit faith, complete
change of attitude, that heals disease, changes
habit and character. Expectancy of relief and
unquestioned faith in the remedy or the physician are much more healing potencies than
either the remedy or the physician. Faith in
the physician, in the reputation of the remedy,
faith in the change of climate, play a tremendous part in the healing, restorative processes.

Faith has ever been the great miracle worker of the ages. It has endowed a spoonful of water, a bread pill, a black ring, a horse-chestnut carried in the pocket, with marvelous healing powers.

Think of the tremendous curative force in the faith of the people who make pilgrimages of thousands of miles on foot to some shrine, often barefooted, and lacerating themselves because of their belief in the beneficence of it to heal! Think of the power to heal of the blind, superstitious faith of those who sacrifice property, sometimes children, almost life itself to get what they regard as the miraculous power of some sacred healing water, as of the Jordan or some of the sacred Eastern rivers, like the Ganges!

Those poor deluded people do not realize that there is no power whatever in these inanimate objects to give them health, but that they take the healing power with them in their faith and might just as well exercise it upon themselves at home.

Inventors who for years battled with poverty and poor health and the opposition of those who did not understand them have completely recovered their health by a sudden discovery of the great secret for which they had so long been struggling. The success of an idea, the sudden achievement which comes after many years of struggling with poverty and discouragement, completely changes their whole physical condition.

Success itself, especially after great disappointment, failure, and poverty, is a tremendous tonic, changing the chemical composition of the secretions and affecting all the functions of the body.

I have known whole families, where discouragement, failure, and sickness had followed them for years, to be transformed by sudden, unexpected success coming to them.

The reverse of this is also true. Unexpected failure, sudden reverses which sweep away fortunes, great sorrows which dishearten and discourage, have often been known to depress and entirely destroy health and happiness.

The physical is merely the outpicturing, the expression, of the mental condition. The condition of our health is our objectified thought.

It will not be long before mental medicine will be recognized as a real science, infinitely more scientific than the present medical system.

For ages man has searched the earth for mineral and vegetable remedies which would

cure his ills, when all the time without knowing it he has had stored in his own brain, in the
depths of his being, the sovereign panacea for
all his aches and pains, a divine harmony which
would antidote all his discords.

The coming physician will teach his patient
that life does not depend upon chance or a cruel
fate, but that there is one steady, persistent,
beneficent purpose, leavening and running
through all creation, and that this purpose is
ever moving upward and onward in one
eternal progression.

For years there has been a gradual, persistent, and progressive falling-off in the use of
drugs, medicine, and many of the old-time
remedies. Statistics show that in one of the
largest cities the prescription business fell off
fifty per cent. within a very few years. People are not drugging themselves as formerly.

A magazine writer estimates that there are
more than fifteen millions of people who do not
believe in medicines and who resort to drugless
healing. Ten years hence, judging from the
rate of increase during the last few years,
there will be fifty millions.

Dr. E. S. Jones, of Boston University, says
in the " American Journal of Clinical Medicine " that unless they adopt the new treatment,

the doctors will be out of business in twenty years' time.

The tremendous reaction from the old-time medical methods is already beginning to be reflected in many of the best medical schools in this country, where instruction is being given by eminent lecturers in mental therapeutics.

The European medical schools are also giving lectures and instructions upon mental medicine. In fact, some of the very medical journals which have shown such bitter hostility to the drugless treatment are now seriously debating its adoption.

Many regular physicians are gradually recognizing mental healing and employing it. A noted nerve specialist now instructs his patient to thoroughly relax his muscles and nerves at certain periods each day and *imagine a vigorous life current flowing through his entire system.*

There is more and more a tendency to use the mind cure *in a strictly scientific sense.* We are recognizing that it is not the drugs, but the Power which created us which heals our wounds and hurts, restores us, and heals all our physical discord.

The more intelligent physicians are beginning to see that the healing of the body is brought about by connecting the patient with the great life storage batteries, with the very Source of Life, the life principle itself.

The future physician will be a man trained to help the sufferer find his God, his good. Then he will need no other remedy.

Love is the normal law of our being, and any departure from the love thought must result in anarchy of the physical economy, because the law of our being has been violated.

All men can rid themselves of their pernicious thought-enemies, enemies of the mind and body, if they will take the trouble to do so.

It is not difficult to shut out poisonous thoughts from the mind. All one need do is to substitute the opposite thought to that which produces the fatal poison, for it will always furnish the antidote. Discord can not exist in the presence of harmony. The charitable thought, the love thought, will very quickly kill the jealousy, the hate, and the revenge thought. If we force pleasant, cheerful pictures into the mind, the gloomy, "blue" thoughts will have to get out.

When we shall have learned to shut out all the enemies of our health, of our digestion, of our assimilation, the enemies which poison our blood and other secretions; when we shall have learned how to keep the imagination clean, the thought pure, the ideals bright; when we shall have learned the tremendous power of a great life-purpose to systematize and purify the life, then we shall know how to live. When we shall have learned to antidote the hate thought, the jealousy thought, the envy, the revenge thought, with the love, the charity thought; when we shall have grasped the secret of antidoting all discordant thoughts with the harmony thought; when we shall have learned the mighty life-giving power in the holding of the right mental attitude and the awful tragedy and suffering which come from holding the wrong mental attitude, then will civilization go forward by leaps and bounds.

Opinions of
The Miracle of Right Thought

Dr. Sheldon Leavitt says:

" I wish to state that I am unusually well pleased with Dr. Marden's 'Miracle of Right Thought.' It is the best work of the author."

Ralph Waldo Trine says:

" This is one of those inspiring, reasonable and valuable books that are bringing new life and new power to so many thousands all over our country and all over the world to-day."

"You have formulated a philosophy

which must sooner or later be universally accepted. Your book shows how the right mental attitude helps one in the realization of every laudable ambition, and the value of cultivating a bright, self-reliant habit of thought. I congratulate you on it."

G. H. SANDISON, *Editor*, *The Christian Herald*.

"It is marked by sanctified common sense

it is in line with the advance thought of to-day, and yet it is so simple in statement that unlettered men and untrained youtns can master its best thoughts and translate them into their daily lives."

REV. R. S. MACARTHUR, D.D., *New York City*.

Rev. F. E. Clark, President United Society of Christian Endeavor, says:

"I regard 'The Miracle of Right Thought' as one of Dr. Marden's very best books, and that is saying a great deal. He has struck the modern note of the power of mind over bodily conditions in a fresh and most interesting way, while he has not fallen into the mistake of some New Thought writers of eliminating the personal God from the universe. No one can read this book sympathetically, I believe, without being happier and better."

Press Reviews of Dr. Marden's
Be Good to Yourself

"The author is a wonder,—

one of the very best preachers, through the pen, of our time."   *Zion's Herald.*

"Just such a discussion of personality

as we all need.   The titles of the chapters are appetizing and the advice and lessons taught are good.   It will help many a reader to understand himself better."
The Advance.

"The kind counsel of a new book

by Orison Swett Marden, who says there are many people who are good to others but not to themselves. This is a fine volume from every point of view."
The Religious Telescope.

"Of a thoroughly inspirational character,

these essays are calculated to awaken and sustain the right sort of ambition and evolve a manly type of character.   They are surcharged with faith, optimism, and common sense."   *The Boston Herald.*

"Dr. Marden's friends,

who are to be found in all quarters of the globe, wait eagerly for such advice as this, on how to be happy, hearty, and healthy."   *Seattle Post-Intelligencer.*

Letters to Dr. Marden concerning
Every Man a King

Success vs. Failure

"One of the most inspiring books I have ever read. I should like to purchase a thousand and distribute them, as I believe the reading of this book would make the difference between success and failure in many lives." CHAS. E. SCHMICK, *House of Representatives, Mass.*

Worth One Hundred Dollars

"I would not take one hundred dollars for your book, 'Every Man a King,' if no other were available." WILLARD MERRIAM, *New York City.*

Unfailing Optimism

"The unfailing note of optimism which rings through all your works is distinctly sounded here." W. E. HUNTINGTON, *Pres., Boston University.*

The Keynote of Life

"'Every Man a King' strikes the keynote of life. Any one of its chapters is well worth the cost of the book." E. J. TEAGARDEN, *Danbury, Conn.*

Simply Priceless

"I have just read it with tremendous interest, and I frankly say that I regard it as simply priceless. Its value to me is immeasurable, and I should be glad if I could put it in the hands of every intelligent young man and woman in this country." CHAS. STOKES WAYNE, *Chappaqua, N. Y.*

Renewed Ambition

"I have read and re-read it with pleasure and renewed ambition. I shall ever keep it near at hand as a frequent reminder and an invaluable text-book." H. H. WILLIAMS, *Brockton, Mass.*

Letters to Dr. Marden concerning
He Can Who Thinks He Can

Will Do Amazing Good

"I believe 'He Can Who Thinks He Can,' comprising some of your editorials, which appear akin to divine inspiration in words of cheer, hope, courage and success, will do amazing good."

JAMES PETER, *Independence, Kas.*

Greatest Things Ever Written

"Your editorials on the subjects of self-confidence and self-help are the greatest things ever written along that line." H. L. DUNLAP, *Waynesburg, Pa.*

Gripping Power

"Presents the truth in a remarkably clear and forcible manner, with a gripping power back of the writing. It is beautiful and inspiring."

C. W. SMELSER, *Coopertown, Okla.*

Beginning of My Success

"Your editorials have helped me more than any other reading. The beginning of my success was when I commenced to practise your teachings."

BRUCE HARTMAN, *Honolulu, T. H.*

Wishes to Reprint It

"I have been very much impressed by the chapter on 'New Thought, New Life.' I would like to send a copy of it to two thousand of my customers, giving due credit of course." JOHN D. MORRIS, *Philadelphia, Pa.*

Full of Light and Joy

"I have studied the subject of New Thought for ten years, but have never seen anything so comprehensive, so full of light and joy, as your treatment of it. When I think of the good it will do, and the thousands it will reach, my heart rejoices."

LOUISE MARKSCHEFFEL, *Toledo, O.*

Letters to Dr. Marden concerning

Pushing to the Front

What President McKinley Said

"It cannot but be an inspiration to every boy or girl who reads it, and who is possessed of an honorable and high ambition. Nothing that I have seen of late is more worthy to be placed in the hands of the American youth." WILLIAM MCKINLEY.

An English View

"I have read 'Pushing to the Front' with much interest. It would be a great stimulus to any young man entering life." SIR JOHN LUBBOCK.

A Powerful Factor

"This book has been a powerful factor in making a great change in my life. I feel that I have been born into a new world."
ROBERT S. LIVINGSTON, *Deweyville, Tex.*

The Helpfulest Book

"'Pushing to the Front' is more of a marvel to me every day. I read it almost daily. It is the helpfulest book in the English language."
MYRON T. PRITCHARD, *Boston, Mass.*

A Practical Gift

"It has been widely read by our organization of some fifteen hundred men. I have personally made presents of more than one hundred copies."
E. A. EVANS, *President Chicago Portrait Co.*

Its Weight in Gold

"If every young man could read it carefully at the beginning of his career it would be worth more to him than its weight in gold." R. T. ALLEN, *Billings, Mon.*

OPINIONS OF
Rising in the World

"**A storehouse of incentive,**
a treasury of precious sayings; a granary of seed-thoughts capable, under proper cultivation, of a fine character harvest."—EDWARD A. HORTON.

"**A stimulating book**
which is pitched at a high note and rings true."
—EDWIN M. BACON.

"**Has all the excellences of style**
and matter that gave to 'Pushing to the Front' its signal success. Dr. Marden's power of pithy statement and pertinent illustration seems inexhaustible."—W. F. WARREN,
Former President of Boston University.

Touches the Springs of Life
"Dr. Marden has touched the springs of life and set forth with marvellous and convincing power the results obtained by those inspired by high resolves, lofty aspirations, and pure motives. No one can rise from reading this book without cleaner desires, firmer resolutions, and sublime ambition."—MYRON T. PRITCHARD,
Master of Everett School, Boston.

Its Immortal Possibilities
"Has the same iron in the blood, the same vigorous constitution, the same sanguine temperament, the same immortal possibilities as 'Pushing to the Front.'"—THOMAS W. BICKNELL,
Ex-U. S. Commissioner of Education.

PRESS REVIEWS OF
The Young Man Entering Business

"A readable volume

on a substantial topic, which discusses actual questions. The counsel of an experienced person." *Pittsburgh Post.*

Abounds in Specific Advice

" We can easily conceive that a young man who gets this book into his hands may, in after life, date his success from reading it. It is sound, wholesome, stimulating. The treatment is concrete. It abounds in specific advice and telling illustration." *Southern Observer.*

Stimulates and Encourages

" Packed as it is with sensible, practical counsels, this volume can be cordially recommended to stimulate and encourage young men starting out in business life." *Brooklyn Times.*

A Necessity to Earnest Young Men

"There is such a thing as the science of success. Dr. Marden has made a study of it. He writes in simple, attractive style. He deals with facts. The book should be in the hands of every earnest young man." *Christian Advocate.*

Entertaining as Well as Helpful

" So interwoven with personal incident and illustration that it is an entertaining as well as a helpful book." *Christian Observer.*

Opinions and Reviews of Dr. Marden's

The Secret of Achievement

Exasperating

"'The Secret of Achievement' is one of those exasperating books which you feel you ought to present to your young friends, yet find yourself unwilling to part with." WILLIAM B. WARREN, *Former President Boston University*.

Art of Putting Things

I have studied Dr. Marden's books with deep interest. He has the art of putting things; of planting in the mind convictions that will live. I know of no works that contain equal inspiration for life."
HEZEKIAH BUTTERWORTH.

A Great Service

"I thoroughly feel that you are rendering a great service to young men and women in America and throughout the world."
REV. R. S. MACARTHUR, D. D., *New York City*.

The Difference

"'Pushing to the Front' is a great book and 'Rising in the World' is a magnificent book, but 'The Secret of Achievement' is a superb book."

Success against Odds

"This volume contains a series of stimulating anecdotes and advice showing how energy, force of well-directed will, application, lofty purpose, and noble ideals serve to win success even against the greatest odds. Many a young man will draw inspiration from it which will aid him in making his life work a success."
School Journal.

OPINIONS OF

𝔗raining for 𝔈fficiency

Practical Ideas

"Dr. Marden has practical ideas, and the suggestions made are good." *Providence Journal.*

Something for Every One

"There is something here for every one. The author goes to bed-rock principles that may apply in the lives of all. The book should be circulated widely." *Milwaukee Journal.*

Radiates Optimism

"The very chapter topics radiate optimism. Every theory enunciated is practical, and the author's views of life deserve to be highly commended." *Christian Endeavor World.*

Sure to Appeal

"The advice given is sound, homely, but sure to appeal. Dr. Marden and his publishers have contributed a notable service in issuing this book." *Trenton Sunday Times.*

Standard Literature

"The chapters constitute standard literature on the subjects discussed. No better book for the efficiency student is to be obtained." *Railroad Men.*

For Young and Old

"Exceedingly practical and highly inspirational. Young and old will read it with equal profit and pleasure." *Christian Advocate.*

OPINIONS OF
The Exceptional Employee

Uplifting to Humanity

"I assure you that the present and future generations must look upon such a work as most uplifting to humanity."

CHARLES FRANCIS, *Charles Francis Press,*
New York City.

Fresh Efforts after Reading

"No one will fail to put forth fresh and better directed efforts to work to the front after reading the book." *Good Health.*

The Ladder of Success

"The author writes with a purpose in view; that purpose is found on the topmost rungs of the ladder of success. In order to find the purpose the reader must ascend this ladder. The rest is easy."

Chamber of Commerce Bulletin (Portland, Ore.).

A Wise Investment

"Any one who employs labor where it requires character and intelligence would make a wise investment by presenting his employees a copy of this book. It has been some time since I have read a more wholesome, inspiring, and fascinating volume." J. J. COLE, in *Christian Standard.*

Brimful of Anecdote and Illustration

"The book is not all theory and principle. It is brimful of the anecdote and illustration from actual business life which gives vigor and acceptance to the writer's ideas."

Christian Advocate.

Sun Books
Sun Publishing

Supplement B-4

─────⊙─────

Booklist of these fine Authors:
James Allen
Christian D. Larson
Orison Swett Marden
Ralph Waldo Trine

─────⊙─────

JAMES ALLEN TITLES

ABOVE LIFE'S TURMOIL by James Allen. True Happiness, Immortal Man, Overcoming of Self, Uses of Temptation, Basis of Action, Belief that Saves, Thought and Action, Your Mental Attitude, The Supreme Justice, Use of Reason, Self-Discipline, Resolution, Contentment in Activity, Pleasant Pastures of Peace, Etc. 163p. 5X8. Paperback. ISBN 0-89540-203-3.

ALL THESE THINGS ADDED by James Allen. Entering the Kingdom, Soul's Great Need, At Rest in the Kingdom, The Heavenly Life, Divine Center, Eternal Now, "Original Simplicity", The Might of Meekness, Perfect Love, Greatness and Goodness, and Heaven in the Heart, Etc. 192p. 5X8. Paperback. ISBN 0-89540-129-0.

AS A MAN THINKETH by James Allen. Thought and Character, Effect of Thought on Circumstances, Effect of Thought on Health and the Body, Thought and Purpose, The Thought-Factor in Achievement, Visions and Ideals, Serenity. 88p. 5X8. Paperback. ISBN 0-89540-136-3.

BYWAYS OF BLESSEDNESS by James Allen. Right Beginnings, Small Tasks and Duties, Transcending Difficulties, Hidden Sacrifices, Sympathy, Forgiveness, Seeing No Evil, Abiding Joy, Silentness, Solitude, Understanding the Simple Laws of Life, Happy Endings, Etc. 202p. 5X8. Paperback. ISBN 0-89540-202-5.

1

THE DIVINE COMPANION by James Allen. Truth as Awakener, Truth as Protector, Of Discipline and Purification, Of Purity of Heart, The First Prophecy- Called Awakening, The Fifth Prophecy- Called Transition, The Second Exhortation- Concerning Humility, Instruction Concerning the Great Reality, Discourse Concerning The Way of Truth, Self-Restraint, Etc. 152p. 5X8. Paperback. ISBN 0-89540-329-3.

EIGHT PILLARS OF PROSPERITY by James Allen. Discussion on Energy, Economy, Integrity, Systems, Sympathy, Sincerity, Impartiality, Self-reliance, and the Temple of Prosperity. 233p. 5X8. Paperback. ISBN 0-89540-201-7.

ENTERING THE KINGDOM by James Allen. The Soul's Great Need, The Competitive Laws and the Laws of Love, The Finding of a Principle, At Rest in the Kingdom, And All Things Added. 82p. 5X8. Paperback. ISBN 0-89540-226-2.

FOUNDATION STONES TO HAPPINESS AND SUCCESS by James Allen. Right Principles, Sound Methods, True Actions, True Speech, Equal Mindedness, Good Results. 53p. 5X8. Paperback. ISBN 0-89540-327-7.

FROM PASSION TO PEACE by James Allen. Passion, Aspiration, Temptation, Transmutation, Transcendence, Beatitude, Peace. 64p. 5X8. Paperback. ISBN 0-89540-077-4.

FROM POVERTY TO POWER by James Allen. The Path to Prosperity, Way Out of Undesirable Conditions, Silent Power of Thought, Controlling and Directing One's Forces, Secret of Health, Success, and Power, The Way of Peace, Power of Meditation, Self and Truth, Spiritual Power, Realization of Selfless Love, Entering into the Infinite, Perfect Peace, Etc. 184p. 5X8. Paperback. ISBN 0-89540-061-8.

THE HEAVENLY LIFE by James Allen. The Divine Center, The Eternal Now, "Original Simplicity", Unfailing Wisdom, Might of Meekness, The Righteous Man, Perfect Love, Perfect Freedom, Greatness and Goodness, Heaven in the Heart. 84p. 5X8. Paperback. ISBN 0-89540-227-0.

THE LIFE TRIUMPHANT by James Allen. Faith and Courage, Manliness and Sincerity, Energy and Power, Self-Control and Happiness, Simplicity and Freedom, Right-Thinking and Repose, Calmness and Resource, Insight and Nobility, Man and the Master, and Knowledge and Victory. 114p. 5X8. Paperback. ISBN 0-89540-125-8.

LIGHT ON LIFE'S DIFFICULTIES by James Allen. The Light that Leads to Perfect Peace, Law of Cause and Effect in Human Life, Values- Spiritual and Material, Adherence to Principle, Management of the Mind, Self-Control, Acts and their Consequences, Way of Wisdom, Individual Liberty, Blessing and Dignity of Work, Diversity of Creeds, War and Peace, Brotherhood of Man, Life's Sorrows, Life's Change, Etc. 137p. 5X8. Paperback. ISBN 0-89540-127-3.

MAN: KING OF MIND, BODY AND CIRCUMSTANCE by James Allen. Inner World of Thoughts, Outer World of Things, Habit: Its Slavery and Its Freedom, Bodily Conditions, Poverty, Man's Spiritual Dominion, Conquest: Not Resignation. 55p. 5X8. Paperback. ISBN 0-89540-212-2.

MEN AND SYSTEMS by James Allen. Men and Systems, Work, Wages, and Well-Being, The Survival of the Fittest as Divine Law, Justice in Evil, Justice and Love, Self-Protection- Animal, Human, and Divine, Aviation and the New Consciousness, The New Courage. 149p. 5X8. Paperback. ISBN 0-89540-326-9.

THE MASTERY OF DESTINY by James Allen. Deeds, Character and Destiny, Science of Self-Control, Cause and Effect in Human Conduct, Training of the Will, Thoroughness, Mind-Building and Life-Building, Cultivation of Concentration, Practice of Meditation, Power of Purpose, Joy of Accomplishment. 120p. 5X8. Paperback. ISBN 0-89540-209-2.

MEDITATIONS, A YEAR BOOK by James Allen. "James Allen may truly be called the Prophet of Meditation. In an age of strife, hurry, religious controversy, heated arguments, ritual and ceremony, he came with his message of Meditation, calling men away from the din and strife of tongues into the peaceful paths of stillness within their own souls, where 'the Light that lighteth every man that cometh into the world' ever burns steadily and surely for all who will turn their weary eyes from the strife without to the quiet within." Contains two quotes and a brief commentary for each day of the year. 366p. 5X8. Paperback. ISBN 0-89540-192-4.

MORNING AND EVENING THOUGHTS by James Allen. Contains a separate and brief paragraph for each morning and evening of the month. 71p. 5X8. Paperback. ISBN 0-89540-137-1.

OUT FROM THE HEART by James Allen. Heart and the Life, Nature of Power of Mind, Formation of Habit, Doing and Knowing, First Steps in the Higher Life, Mental Conditions and Their Effects, Exhortation. 54p. 5X8. Paperback. ISBN 0-89540-228-9.

THE SHINING GATEWAY by James Allen. The Shining Gateway of Meditation, Temptation, Regeneration, Actions and Motives, Morality and Religion, Memory, Repetition and Habit, Words and Wisdom, Truth Made Manifest, Spiritual Humility, Spiritual Strength, Etc. 58p. 5X8. Paperback. ISBN 0-89540-328-5.

THROUGH THE GATE OF GOOD by James Allen. The Gate and the Way, Law and the Prophets, The Yoke and the Burden, The Word and the Doer, The Vine and the Branches, Salvation this Day. 66p. 5X8. Paperback. ISBN 0-89540-216-5.

THE WAY OF PEACE by James Allen. The Power of Meditation, The Two Masters: Self and Truth, Spiritual Power, Realization of Selfless Love, Entering into the Infinite, Saints, Sages and Saviors, The Law of Service, Realization of Perfect Peace. 113p. 5X8. Paperback. ISBN 0-89540-229-7.

PERSONALITY: IT'S CULTIVATION AND POWER AND HOW TO ATTAIN by Lily L. Allen. Personality, Right Belief, Self-Knowledge, Intuition, Decision and Promptness, Self-Trust, Thoroughness, Manners, Physical Culture, Mental, Moral and Spiritual Culture, Introspection, Emancipation, Self-Development, Self-Control and Mental Poise, Liberty, Transformation, Balance, Meditation and Concentration. 170p. 5X8. Paperback. ISBN 0-89540-218-1.

CHRISTIAN D. LARSON

BRAINS AND HOW TO GET THEM by Christian D. Larson. Building the Brain, Making Every Brain Cell Active, Principles in Brain Building, Practical Methods in Brain Building, Vital Secrets in Brain Building, Special Brain Development, The Inner Secret, The Finer Forces, Subjective Concentration, Principle of Concentration, Development of Business Ability, Accumulation and Increase, Individual Advancement, The Genius of Invention, The Musical Prodigy, Talent and Genius in Art, Talent and Genius in Literature, Vital Essentials in Brain Building. 233p. 5X8. Paperback. ISBN 0-89540-382-X.

YOUR FORCES AND HOW TO USE THEM by Christian D. Larson. How We Govern the Forces We Possess, The Use of Mind in Pratical Action, Training the Subconscious for Special Results, How Man Becomes What He Thinks, He Can Who Thinks He Can, How We Secure What We Persistently Desire, Concentration and the Power of Suggestion, The Development of the Will, The Building of a Great Mind, How Character Determines Constructive Action, The Creative Forces in Man, Imagination and the Master Mind, Ect. 331p. 5X8. Paperback. ISBN 0-89540-380-3.

ORISON SWETT MARDEN

AMBITION AND SUCCESS by Orison Swett Marden. What is Ambition?, The Satisfied Man, The Influence of Environment, Unworthy Ambitions, Ambition Knows No Age Limit, Make Your Life Count, Visualize Yourself in a Better Position, Thwarted Ambition, Why Don't You Begin?. 75p. 5X8. Paperback. ISBN 0-89540-369-2.

BE GOOD TO YOURSELF by Orison Swett Marden. Be Good to Yourself, Where Does Your Energy Go?, The Strain to Keep Up Appearances, Nature as a Joy Builder, The Right to be Disagreeable, The Good Will Habit, Keeping a Level Head, Getting the Best Out of Employees, Don't Let Your Past Spoil Your Future, The Passion for Achievement, Neglect Your Business But Not Your Boy, The Home as a School of Good Manners, Self Improvement as Investment, Etc. 322p. 5X8. Paperback. ISBN 0-89540-364-1.

CHARACTER - The Grandest Thing in the World by Orison Swett Marden. A Grand Character, The Light Bearers, The Great-Hearted, Intrepidity of Spirit, "A Fragment of the Rock of Ages," Etc. 55p. 5X8. Paperback. ISBN 0-89540-297-1.

CHEERFULNESS AS A LIFE POWER by Orison Swett Marden. What Vanderbilt Paid for Twelve Laughs, The Cure for Americanitis, Oiling Your Business Machinery, Taking Your Fun Every Day as You Do Your Work, Finding What You Do Not Seek, "Looking Pleasant"- A Thing to be Worked From the Inside, The Sunshine Man. 79p. 5X8. Paperback. ISBN 0-89540-363-3.

EVERY MAN A KING or Might in Mind Mastery by Orison Swett Marden. Steering Thought Prevents Life Wrecks, How Mind Rules the Body, Thought Causes Health and Disease, Overcoming Fear, Mastering our Moods, The Power of Cheerful Thinking, Affirmation Creates Power, How Thinking Brings Success, Building Character, The Power of Imagination, How to Control Thought, Etc. 240p. 5X8. Paperback. ISBN 0-89540-334-X.

THE EXCEPTIONAL EMPLOYEE by Orison Swett Marden. The Exceptional Employee, Self-Discovery, Conquering an Uncongenial Environment, The Power of Enthusiasm, Self-Confidence Gets the Job, Why A Good Appearance Wins, Getting the Position That Calls Out Your Best, Health as Business Capital, Putting Your Best into Everything, In Cheating Your Employer You Cheat Yourself, Keeping Your Working Standards Up, Gray Hairs Seeking a Job, All Work and No Play a Bad Policy, Make Your Work Your Masterpiece, Etc. 202p. 5X8. Paperback. ISBN 0-89540-352-8.

GETTING ON by Orison Swett Marden. Who Holds You Down?, A Cheery Disposition, How to Be Popular, Physical Vigor And Achievement, Begin Right- Right Away, Emergencies- the Test of Ability, Go Into Business for Yourself, The Stimulus of Rebuffs, Gentleness Versus Bluster, The Miracle of Polite Persistency, Over-Sensitivness as a Barrier, The Tragedy of Carelessness, The Love of Excellence, A Vacation as an Investment, On Commercializing One's Ability, Mere Money-Making is Not Success, Etc. 325p. 5X8. Paperback. ISBN 0-89540-370-6.

GOOD MANNERS- A PASSPORT TO SUCCESS by Orison Swett Marden. The Home Training, Self-Respect, Self-Control, Tact, The Relation of Courtesy to a Business Career, Manners in Public Life, The Law of Kindness. 64p. 5X8. Paperback. ISBN 0-89540-366-8.

HE CAN WHO THINKS HE CAN by Orison Swett Marden. He Can Who Thinks He Can, Getting Aroused, Education by Absorption, Freedom at Any Cost, What the World Owes to Dreamers, The Spirit in Which You Work, Responsibility Develops Power, Stand for Something, Happy, If Not, Why? Originality, Sizing Up People, Getting Away From Poverty, Etc. 245p. 5X8. Paperback. ISBN 0-89540-346-3.

THE HOUR OF OPPORTUNITY by Orison Swett Marden. The Hour of Opportunity: Are You Ready For It? Self-Made or Never Made, Do Not Wait For Opportunity, Self-Training, Do You Know a Good Thing When You See It?, Every-Day Opportunities, The Executive Quality, What Is My Right Place, "I Never Asked Anything About It," The Power of Adaption, Focus Your Energies, Become a Specialist, The Inspiration of a Great Purpose, Etc. 72p. 5X8. Paperback. ISBN 0-89540-336-6.

HOW THEY SUCCEEDED by Orison Swett Marden. Marshall Field, Alexander G. Bell, Helen Gould, Philip D. Armour, Mary E. Proctor, John Wanamaker, Darius Ogden Mills, Lillian Nordica, John D. Rockefeller, Julia Ward Howe, Thomas A. Edison, Lew Wallace, Andrew Carnegie, John Burroughs, James Whitcomb Riley, Etc. 365p. 5X8. Paperback. ISBN 0-89540-345-5.

HOW TO GET WHAT YOU WANT by Orison Swett Marden. How to Get What You Want, Discouragement a Disease- How to Cure It, The Force that Moves Mountains, Faith and Drugs, How to Find Oneself, How to Attract Prosperity, Heart-to-Heart Talks With Yourself, Etc. 331p. 5X8. Paperback. ISBN 0-89540-335-8.

HOW TO SUCCEED or Stepping Stones to Fame and Fortune by Orison Swett Marden. Seize Your Opportunity, How Did He Begin?, What Shall I Do?, Foundation Stones, The Conquest of Obstacles, To Be Great- Concentrate, Thoroughness, Courage and Will Power, Guard Your Weak Point, Live Upward, Moral Sunshine, Hold Up Your Head, Books and Success, Etc. 332p. 5X8. Paperback. ISBN 0-89540-371-4.

AN IRON WILL by Orison Swett Marden. Training the Will, Mental Discipline, Conscious Power, Do You Believe in Yourself? Will Power in its Relation to Health and Disease, The Romance of Achievement Under Difficulties, Concentrated Energy, Staying Power, Persistent Purpose, Success Against Odds, Etc. 49p. 5X8. Paperback. ISBN 0-89540-283-1.

LITTLE VISITS WITH GREAT AMERICANS or Success Ideals and How to Attain Them, Vol. I. by Orison Swett Marden. Thomas Alva Edison, Andrew Carnegie, Marshall Field, John Wanamaker, Darius Ogden Mills, Cornelius Vanderbilt, Samuel Gompers, Theodore Roosevelt, Nelson A. Miles, Jacob Gould Shurman, James Witcomb Riley, Ella Wheeler Wilcox, Lew Wallace, Mrs. Burton Harrison, Edwin Austin Abbey, Alice Barber Stevens, Frederic Remington, Charles Dana Gibson. Etc. 352p. 5X8. Paperback. ISBN 0-89540-372-2.

LITTLE VISITS WITH GREAT AMERICANS or Success Ideals and How to Attain Them, Vol. II. by Orison Swett Marden. Frederick Burr Opper, Marshall P. Wilder, Richard Mansfield, John Philip Sousa, Helen Keller, John Burroughs, Helen Miller Gould, Nathan Strauss, Robert Collyer, Lillian Nordica, Etc. Canadians: Robert Laird Borden, S.N. Parent, Andrew G. Blair, Sir William C. VanHorne, Etc. 389p. 5X8. Paperback. ISBN 0-89540-373-0.

LITTLE VISITS WITH GREAT AMERICANS or Success Ideals and How to Attain Them, TWO VOLUME SET by Orison Swett Marden. 741p. 5X8. Paperback. ISBN 0-89540-374-9.

MAKING LIFE A MASTERPIECE by Orison Swett Marden. Making Life a Masterpiece, Practical Dreamers, Where Your Opportunity Is, The Triumph of Common Virtues, Masterfulness and Physical Vigor, Curing the Curse of Indecision, Unlocking Your Possibilities, The Will to Succeed, The Kingship of Self Control, Finding Your Place, The Secret of Happiness, Etc. 329p. 5X8. Paperback. ISBN 0-89540-365-X.

THE MIRACLE OF RIGHT THOUGHT by Orison Swett Marden. Working for One Thing and Expecting Something Else, Expect Great Things of Yourself, Self-Encouragement by Self-Suggestion, Change the Thought- Change the Man, The Paralysis of Fear, Getting in Tune, A New Way of Bringing Up Children, Training for Longevity, As A Man Thinketh, Etc. 339p. 5X8. Paperback. ISBN 0-89540-311-0.

THE OPTOMISTIC LIFE by Orison Swett Marden. The Power of Amiability, The Inner Life as Related to Outward Beauty, The Value of Friends, The Cost of an Explosive Temper, Learn to Expect a Great Deal of Life, Mental Power, If You Can Talk Well, Brevity and Directness, What Distinguishes Work From Drudgery, Keeping Fit for Work, Mastering Moods, Business Integrity, Wresting Triumph from Defeat, Freshness in Work, Don't Take Your Business Troubles Home, Let It Go, Etc. 316p. 5X8. Paperback. ISBN: 0-89540-351-X.

PEACE, POWER, AND PLENTY by Orison Swett Marden. The Power of the Mind to Compel the Body, Poverty a Mental Disease, The Law of Opulence, Character-Building and Health-Building During Sleep, Health Through Right Thinking, Imagination and

Health, How Suggestion Influences Health, Why Grow Old?, The Miracle of Self-Confidence, Self-Control vs the Explosive Passions, Good Cheer- God's Medicine, Etc. 323p. 5X8. Paperback. ISBN 0-89540-343-9.

THE POWER OF PERSONALITY by Orison Swett Marden. What a Good Appearance Will Do, The Essentials of a Good Appearance, Cleanliness and Morals, The Importance of Dress, "The Manners Make the Man," Hindering Habits, Shyness, Personal Magnetism. 86p. 5X8. Paperback. ISBN 0-89540-362-5.

PUSHING TO THE FRONT VOL I by Orison Swett Marden. Opportunities Where You Are, Possibilities in Spare Time, How Poor Boys and Girls Go to College, Your Opportunity Confronts You-What, Will You Do With It?, Choosing a Vocation, Concentrated Energy, The Triumph of Enthusiasm, Promptness, Appearance, Personality, Common Sense, Accuracy, Persistence, Success Under Difficulties, Observation and Self-Improvement, The Triumph of the Common Virtues, Etc. 432p. 5X8. Paperback. ISBN 0-89540-331-5.

PUSHING TO THE FRONT VOL II by Orison Swett Marden. The Man With an Idea, The Will and the Way, Work and Wait, The Might of Little Things, Expect Great Things of Yourself, Stand for Something, Habit: The Servant or The Master, The Power of Purity, The Power of Suggestion, The Conquest of Poverty, The Home as a School of Good Manners, Thrift, Why Some Succeed and Others Fail, Character is Power, Rich Without Money, Etc. 441p. 5X8. Paperback. ISBN 0-89540-332-3.

PUSHING TO THE FRONT, TWO VOL. SET by Orison Swett Marden. 873p. 5x8. Paperback. ISBN: 0-89540-333-1

RISING IN THE WORLD or ARCHITECTS OF FATE by Orison Swett Marden. Dare, The Will and the Way, Uses of Obstacles, Self-Help, Work and Wait, Rich Without Money, Opportunities Where You Are, The Might of Little Things, Choosing a Vocation, The Man With an Idea, The Curse of Idleness, Etc. 318p. 5X8. Paperback. ISBN 0-89540-375-7.

THE SECRET OF ACHIEVEMENT by Orison Swett Marden. Moral Sunshine, "Blessed Be Drudgery", Honesty- As Principle and As Policy, Habit: The Servant or The Master, Courage, Self-Control, & The School of Life, Decide, Tenacity of Purpose, The Art of Keeping Well, Purity is Power, Etc. 301p. 5X8. Paperback. ISBN 0-89540-337-4.

SELF-INVESTMENT by Orison Swett Marden. If You Can- Talk Well, Put Beauty into Your Life, Enjoying What Others Own, Personality as a Success Asset, How to Be a Social Success, The Miracle of Tact, "I Had a Friend," Ambition, Education by Reading, Discrimination in Reading, Reading- A Spur to Ambition, The Self-Improvement Habit- A Great Asset, The Raising of Values, Self-Improvement Through Public Speaking, What a Good Appearance Will Do, Self-Reliance, Mental Friends and Foes. 315p. 5X8. Paperback. ISBN 0-89540-376-5.

SELLING THINGS by Orison Swett Marden. The Man Who Can Sell Things, Training the Salesman, Making a Favorable Impression, The Selling Talk or "Presentation", How to Get Attention, Friend-Winner and Business-Getter, Sizing Up the Prospect, How Suggestion Helps in Selling, The Gentle Art of Persuasion, Closing the Deal, Enthusiasm, Meeting and Forestalling Objections, Finding Customers, When You are Discouraged, Know Your Goods, Character is Capital, Keeping Fit and Salesmanship, Etc. 276p. 5X8. Paperback. ISBN 0-89540-339-0.

SUCCESS, A BOOK OF IDEALS, HELPS, AND EXAMPLES FOR ALL DESIRING TO MAKE THE MOST OF LIFE by Orison Swett Marden. Enthusiasm, Education Under Difficulties, The Game of the World, Misfit Occupations, Doing Everyting to a Finish, "Help Yourself Society," "I Will," Conduct as Fine Art, Character Building, Medicine for the Mind, "This One Thing I Do," "I Had a Friend," Ideals. 347p. 5X8. Paperback. ISBN: 0-89540-360-9.

SUCCESS NUGGETS by Orison Swett Marden. Does an Education Pay?, To Take the Drudgery Out of Your Occupation, Where Happiness is Found, Why He Was Not Promoted, Why They Are Poor, Why He Found Life Disappointing, If You Would Be Very, Very Popular, What the World Wants, Don't Wait for Your Opportunity-Make It, When is Success a Failure?, He Succeeded in Business but Failed as a Man Because..., Does a Vacation Pay?, What Message Does Your Success Bring?, The Time Will Come, Etc. 76p. 5X8. Paperback. ISBN: 0-89540-354-4.

THE VICTORIOUS ATTITUDE by Orison Swett Marden. The Victorious Attitude, "According to Thy Faith," Making Dreams Come True, Making Yourself a Prosperity Magnet, The Triumph of Health Ideals, How to Make the Brain Work for Us During Sleep, Preparing the Mind For Sleep, How to Stay Young, Our Oneness With Infinite Life, Etc. 358p. 5X8. Paperback. ISBN: 0-89540-353-6.

WHY GROW OLD? by Orison Swett Marden. Marden instructs his reader to "hold to youthful, buoyant thought" and keep the imagination alive and flexible. Recognizing that we may be slaves to our attitudes, this text encourages us to make as much of ourselves as possible and in doing so watch as our lives are prolonged. 30p. 5X8. Paperback. ISBN 0-89540-340-4.

WINNING OUT by Orison Swett Marden. Good Manners and Success, Learning to Hold Your Tounge, The Emperor Who Earned

His Own Shoe-Leather, The Boy Who Did Not Know What Time It Was, The Golconda Diamonds, Heroic Youth, The Story of the Little Red Violin, Gold Dust, Seven Hundred Books and the Farm Boy, Training for the Presidency, Send Us a Man Who Can Swim, Abraham Lincoln's Advice About Schooling, Where Does the Fun Come In?. Etc. 251p. 5X8. Paperback. ISBN 0-89540-377-3.

YOU CAN, BUT WILL YOU? by Orison Swett Marden. The Magic Mirror, The New Philosophy of Life, Connecting With the Power that Creates, You Can, But Will You?, How Do You Stand With Yourself?, The New Philosophy in Business, What Are You Thinking?, Facing Life the Right Way, How to Realize Your Ambition, The Open Door, Do You Carry Victory in Your Face? Etc. 338p. 5X8. Paperback. ISBN 0-89540-342-0.

THE YOUNG MAN ENTERING BUSINESS by Orison Swett Marden. Personal Capital and Choosing a Vocation, Avoid Misfit Occupations, Fixity of Purpose, When It Is Right to Change, Personal Appearance, Manners, Sensitivness and Success, The Power of Decision, The Value of Business Training, Promotion from Exceptional Work, The Timid Man and Self-Confidence, Born to Conquer, Getting to the Point, Looking Well an Keeping Well, Salesmanship, System and Order, Shall I Go Into Business for Myself?, Tact and the Art of Winning, People's Confidence, Other Men's Brains, The Art of Advertising, Keeping Up With the Times, Friendship and Success. Etc. 307p. 5X8. Paperback. ISBN 0-89540-378-1.

RALPH WALDO TRINE

CHARACTER BUILDING THOUGHT POWER by Ralph Waldo Trine. "Have we within our power to determine at all times what types of habits shall take form in our lives? In other words, is habit-forming, character-building, a matter of mere chance, or do we have it within our control?" 51p. 5X8. Paperback. ISBN 0-89540-251-3.

EVERY LIVING CREATURE or Heart Training Through the Animal World, by Ralph Waldo Trine. "The tender and humane passion in the human heart is too precious a quality to allow it to be hardened or effaced by practices such as we often indulge in." *Ralph Waldo Trine.* 50p. 5X8. Paperback. ISBN 0-89540-309-9.

THE GREATEST THING EVER KNOWN by Ralph Waldo Trine. The Greatest Thing Ever Known, Divine Energies in Every-Day Life, The Master's Great but Lost Gift, The Philosopher's Ripest Life Thought, Sustained in Peace and Safety Forever. 57p. 5X8. Paperback. ISBN 0-89540-274-2.

THE HIGHER POWERS OF MIND AND SPIRIT by Ralph Waldo Trine. The Silent, Subtle Building Forces of Mind and Spirit, Thought as a Force in Daily Living, The Divine Rule in the Mind and Heart, The Powerful Aid of the Mind in Rebuilding Body-How Body Helps Mind, Etc. 240p. 5X8. Paperback. ISBN 0-89540-278-5.

IN THE FIRE OF THE HEART by Ralph Waldo Trine. With the People: A Revelation, The Conditions that Hold among Us, As Time Deals with Nations, As to Government, A Great People's Movement, Public Utilities for the Public Good, Labour and Its Uniting Power, Agencies Whereby We Shall Secure the People's Greatest Good, The Great Nation, The Life of the Higher Beauty and Power. 336p. 5X8. Paperback. ISBN 0-89540-310-2.

IN THE HOLLOW OF HIS HAND by Ralph Waldo Trine. The Present Demand to Know the Truth, The Thought- The Existing Conditions- and theReligions of Jesus' Time, What Jesus Realized, Jesus' Own Statement of the Essence of Religion, Was the Church Sanctioned or Established by Jesus?, Our Debt to the Prophets of Israel, The Power- The Beauty- and the Sustaining Peace. 242p. 5X8. Paperback. ISBN 0-89540-358-7.

THE MAN WHO KNEW by Ralph Waldo Trine. The Power of Love, All is Well, That Superb Teaching of "Sin", He Teaches the Great Truth, When a Brave Man Chooses Death, Bigotry in Fear Condemns and Kills, Love the Law of Life, The Creative Power of Faith and Courage, Etc. 230p. 5X8. Paperback. ISBN 0-89540-267-X.

MY PHILOSOPHY AND MY RELIGION by Ralph Waldo Trine. This Place: Amid the Silence of the Centuries, With the Oldest Living Things, My Philosophy, My Religion, The Creed of the Open Road. 130p. 5X8. Paperback. ISBN 0-89540-349-8.

THE NEW ALIGNMENT OF LIFE by Ralph Waldo Trine. Science and Modern Research, The Modern Spiritual Revival, The Vitilising Power of the Master's Message, Modern Philosophic Thought, A Thinking's Man Religion, A Healthy Mind in a Healthy Body, The Mental Law of Habit. 228p. 5X8. Paperback. ISBN 0-89540-347-1.

ON THE OPEN ROAD by Ralph Waldo Trine. "To realize always clearly that thoughts are forces, that like creates like and like attracts like, and that to determine one's thinking therefore is to determine his life." 65p. 5X8. Paperback. ISBN 0-89540-252-1.

THIS MYSTICAL LIFE OF OURS A Book of Suggestive Thoughts for Each Week Through the Year by Ralph Waldo Trine. The Creative Power of Thought, The Laws of Attraction, Prosperity, and Habit-Forming, Faith and Prayer- Their Nature, Self-Mastery,

Thoughts are Forces, How We Attract Success or Failure, The Secret and Power of Love, Will- The Human and The Divine, The Secret of the Highest Power, Wisdom or Interior Illumination, How Mind Builds Body, Intuition: The Voice of the Soul, To Be at Peace, Etc! 190p. 5X8. Paperback. ISBN 0-89540-279-3.

THROUGH THE SUNLIT YEAR by Ralph Waldo Trine. A book of Suggestive Thoughts for each day of the year from the writings of Ralph Waldo Trine. 250p. 5X8. Paperback. ISBN 0-89540-350-1.

WHAT ALL THE WORLD'S A-SEEKING by Ralph Waldo Trine. The Principle, The Application, The Unfoldment, The Awakening, The Incoming, Character-Building Thought Power. 224p. 5X8. Paperback. ISBN 0-89540-359-5.

THE WINNING OF THE BEST by Ralph Waldo Trine. Which Way is Life Leaning?, The Creative Power of Thought, The Best Is the Life, The Power That Makes Us What We Are, A Basis of Philosophy and Religion, How We Will Win the Best. 100p. 5X8. Paperback. ISBN 0-89540-348-X.

ELBERT HUBBARD

A MESSAGE TO GARCIA and Other Essays by Elbert Hubbard. A Message to García, The Boy from Missouri Valley, Help Yourself by Helping the House. "He was of big service to me in telling me the things I knew, but which I did not know I knew, until he told me." *Thomas A. Edison.* 48p. 5X8. Paperback. ISBN 0-89540-305-6.

Please write for our *Religions, Oriental, and Western Mysticism Book Catalog,* and our *Motivational and Success Book Catalog* from Sun Publishing Co., P.O. Box 5588-B4, Santa Fe, NM 87502-5588 USA.

Visit our web site at http://www.sunbooks.com/

10 SEP 1997   B-SUPP1.PM5

for notes

for notes

for notes

for notes